40 STEPS

CLOSER TO THE SON

40 STEPS
CLOSER TO THE SON

A practical guide to a closer
relationship with God

James Franciamore

James1:17 Creations
James117Creations.com

40 Steps Closer to the Son
Copyright© 2009 by James Franciamore

Published by James 1:17 Creations
New York, NY

ISBN 978-0-578-02371-7

Library of Congress Control Number: 2009929334

Edited by Mike Valentino
Cover Design by Rajú Hudson – www.ImpaqPrints.com
Photography and Interior design by James Franciamore
with a special thanks to Jose Chavez, Catherine Basilan, Savina Collazo, Franco Rosado, and Nnenna Franciamore

Printed in the United States of America
2nd Printing September 2009

Dedication

"Amen! Praise and glory and wisdom and thanks and honor and power and strength be to our God for ever and ever. Amen!" Revelations 7:12

I have to dedicate this book first and foremost to God. I don't want this to sound like a speech at the Grammy Awards but I really would be nothing without God. So I give the utmost praises to Him. Like my mother-in-law says if my body was filled with mouths, I still wouldn't be able to praise God enough. He is my inspiration, my guiding light, my helper, and my motivation for this book. I could go on forever thanking Him. So I will stop here and say, "Thank you!"

I also have to give a special thanks to two special ladies in my life, my wife, Nnenna, and my daughter, Victoria. Proverbs 18:22 says, "He who finds a wife finds something good". I definitely found something good in my wife. She has supported me throughout my whole journey with God. She has always been my number one fan. I am truly grateful for her. "I thank my God every time I remember you." (Philippians 1:3)

Victoria, when you are old enough to read this, I want you to know that I love you. You gave me joy throughout every page of this book. I could have written about you on each page, instead I chose to allow all the lessons you've taught me as your father to be reflected in my words. As the proverbs say, "You have brought joy to your father". You have taught me so many lessons from being your father. I look forward to seeing you draw closer to God.

1 Thessalonians 3:9 says: How can we thank God enough for you in return for all the joy we have in the presence of our God because of you? I also need to give thanks to my brothers and sisters in the New York City Church of Christ. For all of the men who studied the Bible with me, those who have helped me spiritually, those who lead the various ministries I've been a part of, and a special thanks to the Bronx Campus Ministry where I currently serve. You guys have helped me to be the man of God that I am today. There are too many names to mention. I thank God for placing me in a church where the Bible is the standard and where there are men and women who are trying to put it into practice, mistakes and all.

Finally I thank God for the child that is being knit together in my wife's womb. I heard your heart beating yesterday for the first time. Thank you in advance for all the lessons you will teach me. And I hope my convictions will continue to deepen and grow, so I can be the example God called me to be for you.

5/23/2009

James Franciamore

Preface

It is a great accomplishment for me to write this book. First of all I hate to read, and second of all I hate to write, but I do know that reading is an essential way to draw closer to God. So my goal was to write some things for myself that I would be able to read easily, but also inspire my relationship with God. So one main goal of was to break down the book into any easy to read format. Here is how it is broken up:

Each chapter or step is divided into 4 pages: 1 introduction page, 2 pages of content and 1 page of questions and scriptures for you to do your own reflection on the topic. *Hopefully you will be able to read two pages in one sitting.* The book is also broken up into 7 sections:

1-7- Primary thoughts about God and your relationship with Him
8-10 Principles of His Son and your response to Him
11-13 Preparing for sin and living in the Spirit
14-19-Practice of healthy relationships
21-27- Paradoxes of character
28-32- Practical lessons
34-40- Paradise

This book will be most beneficial to you if you are consistent and take the time to read the scripture references on your own. It was constructed to be read as a forty day study, but you can take as much time on each topic as you would like. It would also be helpful to read it with someone else or use it as a group study guide. Discussions with others about personal struggles and victories usually help to cement convictions to your soul.

I hope the book make sense for *you.* People have asked me: *what did you mean by that or what were you trying to say over there.* I ask them, *What do you get out of it?* I see this book as a work of art. I want you to take what you read and make it your own. Put you own thoughts into it, add your own scriptures, or add your own questions. I know there are so many more scriptures I could add or questions I could ask. So I need you to fill in the blanks as the Holy Spirit enables you to.

I can't provide you with a relationship with God. The Holy Spirit has to do that. 2 Corinthians 5:11 tells us, "Since, then, we know what it is to fear the Lord, we try to persuade men." This is all I can do. I can try to persuade you to fear the Lord. Now the fear of the Lord is a good thing. The book of Ecclesiastes ends by saying, "Fear God and keep his commands this is the whole duty of a man." The Spirit will provide you with all that you need to draw close to God. I am here to persuade you to stay on track, because God has a reward for you at the end of the road.

I also hope you can have fun reading this book. Most people don't understand my humor but I hope you enjoy my attempt to be comical. Above all, I hope that you take your relationship with God seriously and give Him your best as you take part with me in this forty step journey. Be strong, take heart, and prepare your minds for what God has in store for you.

Introduction

We live in an age in which we can easily get the material things we want. We want to totally understand everything about the world we live in. We want so much, in fact, that whatever we have is never enough. The things we have get old quickly. We get bored easily. So whatever it is that we want (and most of the time we don't really know what that is) we want it now.

Some of us think about God this way too. *I want it now. Fix me. Hurry up. I'm bored. I need something new. I need something fun.* But we have to understand that God is not like that at all. The more I get to know God, the more I realize how much more I *don't* know about Him. More technology and more scientific discoveries will never bring us a full understanding of God- and many of us don't like that one bit.

So in this book I am not going to tell you that I've figured it out. I am not going to tell you, "Here is a quick fix to all of your problems!" I am just going to tell you it's a journey, a long journey, a *really* long journey.

I just came back from a pretty long morning prayer walk and I was walking towards the rising sun. I took a lot more than forty steps and it still did not seem that I was any closer to it. The prayer time was great but I ended up back in my house when I was finished. So this book does not claim to take you to a place you've never been before. I am not claiming to blow your mind. I just want to take you forty steps closer.

We live on a sphere. There is no beginning and no end to that shape. If you keep walking you will eventually come back to the same place you started from. Chapter 1 in *Ecclesiastes* tells us:

> Generations come and generations go, but the earth remains forever. The sun rises and the sun sets and hurries back to where it rises. The wind blows to the south and turns to the north; round and round it goes, ever returning on its course. All streams flow into the sea, yet the sea is never full. To the place the streams come from, there they return again. All things are wearisome, more than one can say. The eye never has enough of seeing, nor the ear its fill of hearing. What has been will be again, what has been done will be done again; there is nothing new under the sun. Is there anything of which one can say, "Look! This is something new" It was here already, long ago; it was here before our time.

"There is nothing new under the sun" If you found it and love it, somebody else saw it before you. If it is a new place to you it is home for someone else. This book will not add something else. We already have enough and there is nothing more to add. This book will just take you back to the things you know and remind you of those things, so you can put them into practice and glorify God with your life.

We have so many gadgets to communicate with each other-house phones, cell phones, text messages, email, instant messaging, face-book-but it seems that relationships are so much shallower than when we just spoke face to face or wrote letters. We have so many ways to travel, but we still don't know where we are going. There are so many different religions in the world, so many different denominations of Christianity, so many different ideas of worship, but we seem to be the farthest from God as we have ever been.

Again all I want to do is take you forty steps closer. I am not going to give you a new degree. I am not going to give you a new gadget to draw closer to God. I'm going to point out the things that have been there all the time, nothing new. He's been here since the beginning. This is also not the last thing you will learn. We will all face God in the end of time. And it's a different path for everyone who is reading this. Yes it's the same words, but everyone will receive the message differently according to their circumstances. Yes there is only one God, but we each need to have a personal relationship with Him. Yes there is only one way to get to Him, but we are all standing at different points on this earth right now, so each of us walks on his or her own unique path.

I first started writing this book in Newport, Rhode Island. There is an inspirational place called the Cliff Walk. It is a three-and-a-half-mile pathway along the coast where the famous Newport mansions are situated. There is a small segment of the path called the Forty Steps. It is extremely short compared to the seven miles of the rest of the walk but it is a great place to reflect. I encourage any one who is able, to take a trip to visit this beautiful sight. Whether or not you make it to Rhode Island, I hope you can take this time to reflect on the Forty Steps in this book.

The journey has already begun. I don't know where you are. I don't know where you have been. I don't know what your plans are for the day. And I don't know when your journey here on this planet will be over. But I want to help you to get at least forty steps closer. I don't know if that is North, South, East, or West, but I encourage you to go as close as you can. I know it is impossible to stare at the sun or get anywhere near it but we can take a few steps towards it.

So I guess you figured out I'm really not taking you on a journey towards the sun. It's not even the biggest star in the universe. I want you to go on a journey towards God and that's way more out of reach than the sun because we can't even see God. But don't worry, He gives us help, He gives us His Son-- not the sun-- but HIS SON, JESUS CHRIST. When we have no direction or no purpose we can refocus and start taking some steps towards His SON, our Savior, Jesus Christ.

Jesus is the Way. (John 14:6) Let's follow in His footsteps. (1 Peter 2:21) It is a narrow road to walk on, (Matthew 7:14) but it is a straight and secure path (Proverbs 4:11) and it is well lit. (Psalm 119:105)

Contents

In the beginning I reminisce on Genesis.
God created light to separate the days from night.
40 steps about our fight. The 40 wrongs the Creator has made right.
40 hopes and 40 dreams. 40 friends and 40 fiends.
40 days and 40 hours. 40 weaknesses and 40 powers.
40 ups and 40 downs. 40 smiles and 40 frowns.
40 people saying yes and the other 40 saying no,
but these are 40 steps where we will go
These 40 stages written on the next few pages are from the life of James
It's about the God I can't even describe with 40 names
There are many references to the number 40 in God's word
Can you remember all the times you have heard?
It definitely appears over 40 times
and I can use them to support my rhymes
Moses was on the mountain for 40 days
before he gave us the 10 commandments to show God's ways
The Israelites wandered for 40 days and 40 nights
Through that time they grumbled and got into fights
David and Solomon reigned for 40 years
They inspired men and helped them overcome fears
Jesus fasted for 40 days in the desert
And the angels protected Him so He wouldn't get hurt
When He came back a second time He hung around for 40 more
He spoke about the kingdom of God and what would be in store
As you read through this book I hope you have fun
Just a few days of praying and you will soon be done
At the end of your journey I hope you are inspired
You should grow spiritual muscle and you will probably be tired
But don't be afraid, there's no need to worry
Take you time through this voyage there is no need to hurry
Now no matter your status or whatever your age is
You can grow through the Spirit as you flip through the pages
If you're 40 years old and you're over the hill
There is still plenty of time to test and see God's perfect will
Come join with me on this 40 step endeavor
It won't be that long especially if you plan to live forever
As we are ending this poem and reaching the 40th line
I hope you don't hasten and fret cause of time
You have already started on your 40 steps towards God's Son
So we can't start over but lets go back to step one.

SEE

GOD...

= Light

In the beginning God...was hovering over the waters... and God said, "let there be light,"... the light was good... the first day. Genesis 1:1-5

You open your eyes and discover the light
You reach for your mother, holding her tight.
You weep from the joy with all of your might.
You are newly created, ready for flight.
You didn't know color, they were just different shades.
You didn't know fat or how much they weighed.
You didn't know money, it was what Daddy made.
Life was so simple, you were not afraid.

JF

Here we go, let's take the first step. Are you excited? The first step is the most basic. See. Before the light came "the earth was formless and empty, darkness was over the surface of the deep." (Gen 1:2) We can't see dark, empty, formlessness, so God had to make something for us to see. God said let there be light and there was light. That's where we get our first day. And that's where I get the first step.

The word for Genesis comes from the Greek word *Geneseos* which translates into "birth" or "origin" I think that is a good title for the beginning of the Bible, so it is definitely a good thought to spark the first step in this book. When we are born the first thing we do is see and every good thing that we see is from God (James 1:17), it is a gift.

Physically speaking or spiritually speaking life begins with birth. When God created the earth He started with light because He is light. (1 John 1:5) But can we see God? Do we have to see God to believe? How can we see God if the Bible says He is an invisible God. (1 Timothy 1:17)

Seeking the answer I asked a few friends where they see God. These were a few answers: the clouds, hope, my daughter, the mountains, wind, snow, people, love, repentance, storms. The question is, "Where do you see God?" You need to see God if you are going to start a relationship with Him.

He is our maker, our creator, a loving parent, the Lord, a mysterious, miraculous, omnipotent, omniscient, wonderful, merciful, powerful, genius, awesome, incomparable, perfect being. He is the beginning, the middle and the end. So we must start, fill up, and commence with God. He calls Himself I AM among many other names. We are not worthy of calling HIM by any name, so for the sake of this book we will refer to God by any one of the names mentioned in the Bible, but we will primarily refer to Him as God.

The whole purpose of this book is for every reader to draw closer to God. If you don't believe in God, that will be tough, but it shouldn't be too difficult to convince you. None of us have a clear picture of what God looks like in terms of physical appearance. Moses had some encounters with Him, but he never took a picture with his digital camera and posted it on the Internet. Is He black, is He white, is He a "he" or does He even have a bodily form as we know it? None of us have the answers to those questions, regardless of any personal dreams or revelations that some claim to have. God has not yet revealed His true image because we would not be able to handle it. The same way that we can not stare directly at the sun, (one of God's small creations), we are not ready to stare directly at Him. We do have some hints as to what God looks like, Genesis 1:27 tells us we are created in God's image, Colossians 1:15 says Jesus is the reflection of God's glory, and we also have His many creations (1 Timothy 4:4). God doesn't want us to see His physical appearance; He wants us to see His power and love. Here are a few examples.

First, let's look at the Earth that we live on. The Earth's size is perfect. If Earth were smaller, an atmosphere would be impossible, like the planet Mercury. If Earth were larger, its atmosphere would contain free hydrogen, like Jupiter. Earth is the only known planet equipped with an atmosphere of the right mixture of gases to sustain plant, animal and human life.

The Earth is located at precisely the right distance from the sun. The temperature swings from roughly -30 degrees to +120 degrees. If the Earth were any farther away from the sun, we would all freeze. Any closer and we would burn up. Even a small difference in the Earth's proximity to the sun would make life on Earth impossible. The Earth remains this perfect distance from the sun while it rotates around the sun at a speed of nearly 67,000 mph. It is also rotating on its axis, allowing the entire surface of the Earth to be properly warmed and cooled every day.

Second, our moon is the perfect size and distance from the Earth for its gravitational pull. The moon creates important ocean tides and movement so ocean waters do not stagnate, and yet it restrains our massive oceans from spilling over across the continents.

Man, I could go on and on, I taught middle school science this past year and every lesson I taught reminded me of how great God is, from the weather, to different plant and animal life, to microorganisms, to the cosmos in the universe, to the Human body. Our bodies are amazing structures. There is an exhibit here in New York called Bodies and it is amazing. I am impressed with the artists and scientist that put it together, but I am much more impressed with the God that created the human body.

If you don't believe there is a creator behind all of this, I guess you could just put the book down right now and write your story of how the Big Bang is true. It's like saying all the letters on this page fell together on their own to make words. I would be very insulted. I worked very hard on this book. Or it's like saying all the pieces of metal, plastic and microchips fell together to make this computer I am typing on. I think the people at Dell would find that to be a little amusing. So basically there is a God, a creator of all the intricate details in this world as we know it.

If you are bold enough to question God get ready to brace yourself like a man. (Job 38:3) For those of us who can just step outside and be convinced there is God. Hallelujah. For those of you who need more convincing the next step is for you. Well, the next step is for all of us. God didn't create us to be dummies. He gave us a free will. It is normal to question things. We should never take things at face value. Use the next pages to dig deeper into your relationship with God. I hope you *see* what I am saying.

If you are a visual learner and you need to see for yourself, God is ready to show you some new things. You don't have to have blind faith. God wants to show you a clear path and guide your steps.

As we complete our first step towards the Son, I hope you will take time to reflect on your life and your relationship with your creator. Use the Scriptures to dig deeper into God's plan for your life. Let's start with a solid foundation so the rest of our steps will be firm and secure and we will be able to finish the journey set before us.

Where do you see God?

Why do you believe there is God?

What creations can you thank God for today?

1. Job 38- Where were you in the beginning? God tells Job to brace him self like a man then He questions Job for two chapters. The God we worship created everything. He laid the Earth's foundation. He is truly Awesome! (Read chapters 39-41 to see the rest of the questions)

2. Jeremiah 10:23- Tells us this life we live is not ours we get it totally from God. He directs the steps we take.

3. Psalm 139: 1-18- Shows how much God knows us, from inside out we are His masterpiece. Look and see how fearfully and wonderfully you were made.

4. Matthew 10:30- God pays attention to detail. He counts the hairs on your head.

5. Isaiah 42: 5-9- Open your eyes, God is the Lord, He is The Great Alpha, He is "the BEGINNING", He is our Creator.

6. Romans 1:20- We are without excuse. God can be seen clearly.

7. Jeremiah 29: 11- God has plans to prosper not to harm. He has hopes for you.

Pray: That you will see God and help other's to do the same.

Smell

Seek and You will Find

Genesis 1:6-8 And God said let there be expanse... God called the expanse
sky and there was evening and there was morning the second day.

This step comes quickly but it's part of the plan
Your curiosity blossoms "Mommy give me a hand."
Grabbing around, reaching for the expanse
Give me one try, oh please just one chance
Thoughts of confusion, is this just a phase
Chasing approval like a mouse in a maze
Wanting the answers but searching nowhere
I'm out for adventure but I really don't care

JF

Seeing a certain image may spark a memory but adding a scent to it, sharpens the memory, giving it more clarity. The title of this chapter is smell, so I will start off with a topic I talk about a lot, farts, I even mentioned them in my wedding vows. To me passing gas is very interesting, because when most people fart they are typically not disgusted by their own smell, and when they are, it's no question that they have delivered a truly foul odor. When I less a little gas loose around my house my wife always there to reassure me that they stink, but I am not sure if my daughter realizes that a fart has a bad odor yet. Farts are very funny some smell like cheese, some like chopped meat, and some like plain old gas. Now to some this might remind them of a summer BBQ, but those in the nearby smelling vicinity would know it is the stinky smell of a raunchy fart!

Smells can be subject to opinion. Some people smell really bad to others. Perhaps, since they have gotten used to their body odor, they are not negatively affected by it. To one nose, cologne is sweet, and to another it's repulsive. Most of these things have to do with how we grew up. Even Christianity has a different smell to different people. (2 Corinthians 2:11) Like anything else, we have to figure it out.

Have you heard the phrase follow your nose? We all like to sniff around. Most of the time it is not a literal sniff around but figuratively speaking - we search. We use the sense of smell to investigate. *Does this have a pleasant smell? Do I want to touch that? Should I taste this? Maybe I should go there?* We use our nose to know when to say no.

In step one, we see, but when there is no visual image, like a fart, we now go to step two. We smell which is an essential key in our spiritual search. So which ever way you cut the cheese you need step two.

There are many things that look harmless but when we get a chance to come close enough to smell, it can be quite harmful. Like a skunk, I'm sure it looks very cute to a small child. After all it is a nice little furry black animal with a white stripe, but take one whiff and watch out, baby.

But as you know the goal is not to talk about skunks and farts. We are talking about searching for God. God is trying to send us His fragrance through Christ and Christianity. (2 Corinthians 2:14-15) If you can't smell it, or you don't enjoy the smell you will not be able to experience God the way He wants you to. God tells us in Amos 5:4 "Seek Me and live." He wants us to seek Him out so we can experience life.

God is not a trickster. He is not playing a hide n' seek game with you. He puts you in the exact places so that you can seek Him. (Acts 17: 26-28) Matthew 7:10 tells us that if we seek we will find. That doesn't mean, *Oh I looked over there and I ain't seen nuttin.* I believe many people don't want to find God, because the end of Acts 17:28 says *perhaps* reach out for Him and find Him. That's the next step, you have to reach out and touch. Even though He makes it easy, He still gives us free choice.

God is very loving and He knows we are "confused." What I mean by "confused", is lost. It is like the feeling I was trying to capture in

16

the poem. I was at a point in my life where I wanted the answer but I was afraid of the truth. I personally don't like making choices because if I don't choose anything, then I really can't be wrong (I had to ban the phrase 'I'm so confused' from my vocabulary for a while because of this). God comes for guys like me with scriptures like Romans 10:20 and John 15:16, God found us, He chose us. That's not just true for me it's true for everyone.

Romans 3:11 says that "there is no one who understands, no one who seeks God" because we could never really seek God or understand Him without Him seeking us first. But even with that, it still comes down to our decision; we have to make the final choice. We have to set our hearts on seeking God (2 Chronicles 30:19). This happens in the beginning of our walk with God but it also happens daily.

We always have to be searching. We always have to be thinking, because there usually is a better way. If you are a Christian, hopefully you already set your mind on making good choices, but if you want to continue to grow and mature you have to always set your mind on making the best choice.

Life is not boring, especially the Christian life. You never experienced today. It is a brand new day for everyone. You never know what is going to happen and you have to live that way. It is sad to see people who have lost their drive to strive for the best. They may say things like, "Another boring day", "Back to the same routine" or "Here we go again". We should never say things like that especially when given the opportunity to see another day, and have another day to live.

There are endless possibilities from day to day.. You may meet the person who was searching for God and you will change their life for eternity. You may have a conversation with someone that will stop them from committing suicide. You might bump into an old friend that you haven't seen in years. You may witness a horrible tragedy. You may find a valuable object on the floor. Each day has so much in store. Just live!

"Seek the LORD, all you humble of the land, you who do what he commands. Seek righteousness, seek humility; perhaps you will be sheltered on the day of the LORD's anger." Zephaniah 2:3. No matter where you are now or where you started from, you still have an opportunity to seek God. Some beginnings have tainted the way some people search for God but don't let that get in your way. Use it to draw closer to him.

2 Chronicles 15:2 "...The Lord is with you when you are with Him. If you seek Him, He will be found by you but if you forsake Him He will forsake you." Don't give up on seeking God. He will not give up on you. He will also allow you to be lost is you decide you do not want to reach out for Him.

You don't have to settle for the life you have now or feel like you have reached your potential. God is cooking up something great for you. Don't let your past predict your future. God always has greater plans. You just need to find them. Can you smell what our great and awesome God is cooking?

17

What are some childhood memories that stay in your mind?

How do they impact your life today?

What are you searching for now?

1. **Ecclesiastes 11:1-** Cast your bread upon waters, take risks. Put your life out there see what God does with it.

2. **Psalm 139:23-24-** The Lord searches us. Are you allowing Him to look at all of you?

3. **Proverbs 2:3-5-**We need to search for insight. We need wisdom to make good decisions.

4. **Luke 15:3-10-** We search for what is missing. It could be a lost sheep or a lost coin. We all have areas we can grow in no matter where we are in our relationship with God.

5. **Jeremiah 17:10-** God is searching our minds and hearts. What's in there?

6. **Psalm 42: 1-2-** When we are thirsting, we are really searching to be with God and God always fills in the gaps.

7. **Proverbs 3:1-2-** We must keep God's commands in our hearts. That keeps us on the right track.

Pray: That you will seek God and He will search out your heart.

Touch

Experience the Experience

Genesis 1: 9-13 ...And God called the dry ground Land. Then God said let the land produce vegetation, seed bearing plants and trees ... the third day

Wow! Look at that tree that fruit is for me
My desires now strong changing from mild
I'm becoming unclean no longer a child
I'm gaining a lost mind I don't even know
With no self control I'm running the show
I'm going some place and I'm doing some thing
I got a new friend I gave her a ring
I'm running real fast faster than then
Hard pressed on both sides their asking me when
I'm engaged got a wife gonna start a new life

JF

Like many concepts, there are two parts to this step; the good and the bad. Number one, God created everything for us to see, smell touch, and ultimately enjoy. He wants us to experience good things. On the other hand, He created a time and place for everything (Ecclesiastes 3) so if we touch at the wrong time or place we will get hurt.

Step three is touch because on the third day God created land and with that an abundance of things for us to touch and experience. It is a natural desire to touch and feel things because it allows us to connect to them, and although our relationship with God is not based solely on feelings, it is essential to feel close to Him if we want a deep relationship with Him. We have to experience things for ourselves to truly know what they are like.

The steps are connecting more tightly as you read through each chapter. First we take notice by seeing, then the smell helps us to determine if we actually want to touch and experience. Sometimes we just want to experience everything regardless of the smell: the good, the bad and the ugly. Obviously everyone wants to experience good things, but most of us, especially boys, want to touch the bad things too. Perhaps simply out of curiosity, or perhaps we are deceived by the smell and are then tempted to touch.

Consider the following scenarios:

"Don't touch that, it's hot".__ *"It can't be that hot, let me feel it for my self."*

"Don't touch that woman," __ *"She's just an acquaintance, we're just friends"*

"Don't touch those drugs" __ *"I'll just try it once; I can stop whenever I want."*

"Don't touch the fruit of the tree"__ *"It looks so shiny, I want it!"*

We have a bad example in Genesis 3:1-7 that we are all too familiar with. Adam and Eve are deceived by the serpent. So most of us follow that bad example and are easily deceived, even when we know that God says it is wrong. Eve was able to tell the serpent in verse 3 that God said, "Even if you touch this fruit you will die." But most of us still like the bad stuff. We like roller-coasters, getting tossed up and down, getting a headache and throwing up. We like scary movies. We like UFC fighting because we want to see someone get their brains bashed in. We watch a lion devour an elephant on National Geographic and say I can't look away. In a twisted way, we like to experience bad things.

Some things are better left untouched, you are better off taking someone else's word for it. In the case of travel, it would be a positive experience to actually go on your dream vacation. It is one thing to look at the Travel Channel and dream of being at that wonderful tropical island, but there is nothing like having the experience yourself.

Some of us have a really hard time experiencing a full life of worshiping God. We worship many idols that can't do anything for us. (Psalms 115:3) We get so excited about cars, women, movies, clothes, and a whole bunch of other things, but often we don't get excited about righteous experiences that will help us grow and have incredible walk with God. We live in the microwave world; we want everything in less than a minute, but we know microwave food never tastes that good.

I believe some of us need to experience the bad things to appreciate God. That's one main reason why I believe God created good and bad because if everything was good it really couldn't be good because we couldn't compare it to anything bad. It's seems cool and ideal to only know the good like Adam and Eve who felt no shame being naked, but again, God has to be fair to us so He allows us to know both good and evil, and it's up to us to make the choice.

Even when we have a bad experience we can rejoice in it. (1 Peter 1:6-9) Some are not as drastic as others, like choosing the wrong meal at a restaurant. You just won't order it when you go back and you will probably tell your friends about it. Other experiences aren't so easy to get over, like relationships. I didn't have great dating relationships before I became a Christian.

As a teenager I thought I was making the best decisions. Like most teenage boys, I decided that having a girlfriend was a need, and once I had one, I would have to behave in a certain way with her to be considered "the man". Reflecting upon my poor choices and experiences that proved to be incredibly negative, I can see what a dork I really was. I experienced too many things with women that caused grief and regrets that I didn't need to experience, especially as a teenager. Now hopefully I can use those experiences to help others.

Most of us reading this book have had our share of experiences; some worse than others and hopefully that helps us to make better decisions for ourselves today. We can also use the experiences of other people to help us with our decision-making, especially the people of the Bible. We can see what happens when people get drunk. (Gen 20:30-36) We see the results of adultery. (2 Samuel 11) We see the results of lying. (Acts 5) We also see positive results of faith, friendship, and fellowship. So what do I do now? I messed up already but I want to have some positive experiences. Some scars won't be as deep and dark, but others will leave marks that will not go away. I praise my wife because I am her first and only boyfriend. She did not have to go through all of the hurt feelings of having bad relationships. She can have all positive expectations of me and our relationship. For those of us who are not as lucky, don't let that hinder you. You can still Survive and Strive.

God gave us this world to enjoy it. There are consequences when we take advantage of it. Feelings make things exciting not boring. We have to remember that God created all of this for our good. We have to give thanks to Him for that.

So go ahead and touch, feel and experience, but heed the warnings. Some things you are better off having no memories of or sometimes it is just not the right time. Don't be afraid to touch, but before you do consider God, and make decisions out of reverence for Him. If you worship the Creator of the earth, the world is yours. Don't be afraid. Explore, Experience, and Enjoy.

What feels good to you?

What is bad for you even thought it feels good?

What are the righteous things that feel right?

1. **Daniel 12: 2-** Where are you leading your life? Are you leading your life towards death? Do you do shameful things?

2. **Matthew- 18:7-9-** Throw off what hinders. If you have sin it will weigh you down and ultimately lead you to Hell.

3. **ITimothy 6: 11-15-** Flee from sin. We have to serve God and fight the good fight. Do the right thing, so you won't be blamed for wrong.

4 **Galatians 6:7** – God cannot be mocked. You reap what you sow. You get what you give.

5. **Proverbs 19:29-** Mockers will get their punishment. Anyone who does something wrong deserve the repercussions. Thank God for His grace.

6. **Exodus 30:29-** We are preparing for service in God's kingdom. Whatever God touches will be holy. If God touched you He expects you to be Holy.

7. **Psalm 16: 6-** Your boundaries have fallen in pleasant places. God's Spirit tells us when to stop.

Pray: That you will make wise choices that will lead you closer to God.

Taste

Do You Like?

Genesis 1:14-19 And God said, "Let there be lights in the expanse. The Greater light to govern the day and the lesser to govern the night... the 4th day

Turn around can't turn back God cut me some slack

I'm in a mess I created man this is whack

I look all around and see what I've done

Killing my youth I've murdered my son

No remorse just regret of what I've become

My heart is so hard my life's cumbersome

I'm ready already. I'm ready to die

I've already tried why should I try.

I'm mad at my self that's why I cried

I feel all alone I'm standing outside

JF

You can touch something but you don't have to taste it, but for most people that is not possible. Once they are close enough to touch it they want to dive in all the way and taste it. My daughter is a perfect example of that, from when she was just a few months everything she touched went straight into her mouth. That was her way of totally experiencing the object at hand. Clean or dirty, she is going to try and taste it. Thank God my wife and I are around to monitor her or else she would be in serious trouble.

God does the same for us. He monitors us when we are young but when we get older He hopes we would have developed a sense of what is right or wrong and not do certain things. Our daughter has already experienced things she does not like to taste and when presented to her again, she will turn her head away. Most of us had to experience things first, we had to know that they are bad and the sad part is that a lot of those same people, even though they know it is bad keep on tasting again. Perhaps they think it might taste better the next time.

Now most things might taste good at first but the problem usually is the consequence. My dog once ate a sea star I brought home from California. He gobbled that thing up so quickly and it came out of his system just as quick, but more disgusting. We are the same way; we get drunk and have hours of hangovers. We have premarital sex and get STD's and babies out of wedlock. We take drugs and lose jobs and relationships. God wants you to know what is bad for you and not to taste it again.

In working with the youth in my church, I remind them constantly that I don't want them to experience some of the things I had to go through. I recently did a lesson with them on obedience. We looked at Jeremiah 11:1 which teaches about obedience and disobedience. If we obey the covenant, we will enter the land of milk and honey. I'm sure that was one of the best tasting things back then. I guess it is like *dulce de leche* ice cream. On the other hand if we disobey, we will taste the wrath of God.

I'm allergic to pine nuts. Even if my lip touches something made with pine nuts, I start to get itchy. The first time I ate something with pine nuts I was at work. I devoured the pasta dish and although it tasted good while I was eating it, ten minutes later I was filled with hives and I could hardly breathe. My boss sent me home immediately, but when I got home my dad just laughed thinking a simple shower will cure me. We all realized the severity of the experience, when the doctor declared that I was so highly allergic, that another episode could close my throat and I would die. So now that I know that pine nuts can kill me, I stay far away from them. In the same way, when I taste the wrong thing by disobedience, I know God's wrath will not only kill my body but my soul.

I can't understand why people smoke. You have to see it looks so stupid. You have to smell that it stinks. If you touch it, it burns you. Why would you taste it? There are even warnings on the label saying it will kill you, but there are still millions of people who smoke. No matter how high the price goes for cigarettes people will still buy them and smoke them. The worst part is that they are addictive. Once you start you can't stop.

Thomas needed the full experience, he didn't just believe. (John 20:24-28)He said I have to see the scars and I have to feel them. Then Jesus tells him in verse 29 that it is blessed to believe without seeing; that's faith, but most people are more like Thomas, they won't believe until they see. When they do see they want to have the whole experience.

Jesus gives us that opportunity in John 8:31-32. He says if you hold to my teaching you will know the truth, and the truth will set you free. Some people say Christianity doesn't work; it is not real. Jesus sort of gives a money back guarantee. He lets you try His product free of charge. So you can see the results. He actually paid the price for you first because He knows Christianity works.

Some of us try to save others from their suffering by enabling them but some people need to hit rock bottom in order to stop tasting the things that harm them. In the Chemical Recovery Ministry at my church, we talked about how the enabler allows the addict to keep on sinning, and though people need grace and mercy, an enabler allows a person to mess up without consequences. The truth is people need consequences to motivate them to change.

Consequences don't have to be that drastic. You don't have to end up homeless to work on your finances, or divorced to work on your marriage. Learn from the minor conflicts to avoid major ones. Also learn from those who have made the mistake. You don't always have to taste it for yourself.

I have given much advice to people and they didn't follow. When I see them suffering for not heeding advice, I am tempted to say I told you so. I usually don't. I just hope that God will lead them to repentance. Many of us have been at the opposite end of that experience when someone said to you I told you so. I just hope you learned your lesson. It is humiliating to make a mistake but in humility we can learn and grow from the experience.

There are also some great decisions that you made and good habits that you have. Those you can be proud of. Some of us need to go back to some of those good things we tasted. Just remember what you tasted so you don't have to get sick twice. Fool me once shame on you. Fool me twice shame on me.

In Revelations 3:16 the Bible tells us that God will taste us, and He will spit us out if we are lukewarm. God does not want us to be in sin because the wages of sin is death. (Romans 6:23) It will kill us. If it does not kill us right away it will entangle us (Hebrews 12: 1) and choke away our life. We have to watch what we eat. We cannot take in too much evil; it is not good for us. Ecclesiastes 10:1 tells us a little folly outweighs wisdom and honor. Just that little bit of poison might kill us so be careful what you taste.

God wants us to taste good things. He gave us the Garden of Eden when He created the Earth and He also gave us the warnings of what not to eat. He gives us the same encouragement and warnings today. We just need to be obedient so we can enjoy the land of Milk and Honey.

What has left a bad taste in your mouth?

What have you tasted that is good?

Are you tempted to return to your vomit like a dog?

1. Psalm 38- The guilt of our sin burdens us. There are many Psalms that show the effect of sin. It would be good to read this whole Psalm. What would your Psalm sound like?

2. Isaiah 59: 1-2- Our sin hides us from God. He hates sin. He can not be around it.

3. Romans 7:14-25- We are unspiritual and the law shows us sin. It shows us sin so we can see it and change it because the sin will kill us.

4. Hebrews 12:1-11- Sin entangles and God disciplines. Discipline hurts at first but it will help afterwards.

5. James 1:2-8- Consider it joy when you go through trials. Challenges are fine; we just need to grow from them.

6. Psalm 34: 8-12- Taste and see that the Lord is good. God loves giving us good things.

7. 2 Peter 2:22- If you go back to your sin, it is the same as you eating vomit. It's nasty.

Pray: That God will protect you from making foolish choices.

Hear

Do You Hear what I Hear?

Genesis 1:20-23 - And God said, "let the water teem with living creatures and let the birds fly above the earth" - the fifth day

I'm still alive got passed step 4
Awaiting an answer I stand by the door
I'm praying to God but losing my Faith
I can't go nowhere I just got to wait
I leaving for work she going to school
She whispers an invite that's sounding real cool
Pinching my self can this stuff be true
God is real Great what can we do
His timing is perfect an incredible plan
Pondering some thing I must understand

JF

The LORD said, "Go out and stand on the mountain in the presence of the LORD, wait for the LORD is about to pass by." Then a great and powerful wind tore the mountains apart and shattered the rocks before the LORD, but the LORD was not in the wind. After the wind there was an earthquake, but the LORD was not in the earthquake. After the earthquake came a fire, but the LORD was not in the fire. And after the fire came a gentle whisper. When Elijah heard it, he pulled his cloak over his face and went out and stood at the mouth of the cave. Then a voice said to him, "What are you doing here, Elijah?"   1 Kings 19:10-13

God puts it right back on Elijah and He put it right back on us. What do we want, what are we doing here? God is always speaking, we just need to listen to His word. The WORD! The Word is GOD, the Word was with GOD, and the Word is the Bible. (John 1) We are like the birds of the air and the fish of the sea and God is fishing for our souls, we just need to catch on. And God's word is not hard for us to understand, it is for ordinary unschooled men. (Acts 4:13) The question is, "Do you hear God speaking to you?"

One of the most memorable sermons I remember from a Pre-teen Christian Camp was one on "choice". Choice is something we have that no one can take that away from us. God tells us what's right and what's wrong but ultimately we make the choice whether or not to listen.

We live in world full of noise. There is so much to hear, and we choose what to listen to. You can choose your radio station, TV show, friends, church sermon, and so on. If we don't like what we hear we can change the channel or just walk away. But the question is, do you want to hear the truth or do you want to hear what will make you feel good? Will you search for what your itching ears want to hear (2 Timothy 4:3), or will you search for the truth because that will set you free?

It is a little more difficult these days to hear the truth clearly, and not only because of blatant sin. Most of the confusing noise comes from "so called" Christians. Many people preach a different doctrine than what is seen in the scriptures. The legalists won't focus on teaching about God's grace and leave you feeling guilty and the liberalist make God out to be a wimp with no real standard and won't tell you about His wrath. There are also hypocrites who make it really difficult to follow their words because their lives do not match what they say. Whatever the situation is, you can never take what someone says at face value, no matter who it is, no matter how many people say it. You have to be a Berean (Acts 17:11). The truth comes from the Bible. Faith comes from hearing the word of God and although people can share their faith with us they must get the answers from the Bible for it to be TRUTH. I believe if you truly have a sincere, surrendered heart to hear God's word He will fill it with the truth.

This step decides how you will live your life. It could come after seeing because the speed of sound is pretty quick. We hear a lot of things. We just have to know what to choose. Daily we hear things like these *"Try drugs." "You need to be skinny like this." "You need to have this much money."* Do you believe those words and other like those? You will do what you believe. And what you do determines how you will live your life.

The parable of the seeds in Matthew 13 is a great example of people's response to what they hear. This parable is extra cool because it has a clear explanation after the parable. It is evident that God really wants us to understand this one.

The seed is the word of God and the grounds are our hearts or our ears. There are different ways we can receive/hear God's word. The first seed falls on the path. Imagine a path. Most paths today are made of concrete. If we put God's word on a concrete sidewalk in midtown Manhattan during rush hour, it will get trampled on and have no time to develop any type of root.

The second seed fell on rocky ground. Again it is hard, but if the seed falls into a crevice it can begin to grow. This reminds me of an intelligent person. They will start to hear the word of God and take some information from it but since they are already so smart they don't allow the new wisdom to penetrate their hearts. Their hearts are hard. They will never have Deep Roots.

The third one lands in the thorns. If the thorns are growing, that means that this is a heart that is able to grow something but this person is not good at taking care of the crop. To me it is a very difficult thing to take care of a garden. You consistently have to be work on the garden and know what the weeds are. When I grow things in my garden I sometimes don't know which ones are weeds. I allow so many things to grow that nothing gets full attention. God's word always has to get first dibs or else the thorns will take over. You will never experience Spiritual Truth.

The last one seed gets dropped in the good soil. It is soft, it is ready for something to be planted in it, and there is nothing else distracting it. It seems almost impossible to be the good soil, as there are so many other things that can get in the way and the biggest one is our selves. That's why the Bible tells us to be like kids. We have to go back to the mindset that we know nothing because that is the only way that we can really learn something new. When you hear God's word how do you receive it? Are still producing Fresh Fruits?

Sometimes it is very clear. A lot of times we have to wrestle with God, but let me remind you that the Bible is good, it's not always what you want to hear but it is good. You have to read the Bible for yourself and not just live by what the preacher says. You have to study the Bible for yourself. Even when Paul was preaching, the Bereans had to examine, eagerly, every day. They wanted to make sure what they heard became their own convictions.

Get ready and listen to God. I don't know how He will start the conversation but Romans 10:17 says faith comes through hearing. You need to hear God's word to increase your faith. If you are ready to hear God just open up your Bible. Tell me; do you hear God singing to you?

What do you like listening to?

Do you like to hear the truth?

Do you ask a lot of question or seek guidance?

1. **Isaiah 42:6-9-** God calls us. He says He will hold your hand and help you to see. He wants to let us know what's going on.

2. **Deuteronomy 6:3-** God wants us to go to the promise land. He will try to lead you there.

3. **Psalms 119: 33** Let's ask God to teach us how to listen, because we are easily confused.

4. **Job 40: 6-7-** God questions us. What answers do you have for Him?

5. **Matthew 8:1-3-** Are you willing? Jesus is willing to help us.

6. **Hebrew 3:7-** If you hear his voice don't harden your heart. If our hearts are hard we will not be able to hear God.

7. **1 Thessalonians 2:13-** "The word of God which you hear from us" We are spreading God's word. Not ours.

Pray: That you will hear God's voice.

Live

I'm Alive for the very First time

Genesis 1:24-31 God said let us create living creatures, lets us make man in our image"

Show me some answers teach me your word

So many faces it seems so absurd

Out of the dark you earnestly came

I gave out my number you gave me the same

I study the Bible, show me the way

It makes so much sense what can I say

The decision is on me and it seems very clear

Losing my old life and denying the fear

Encouraged by God but discouraged by men

With the Spirit and water I am born again

God creates life so that we can live. Even the smallest, ugliest creature is living and moving. That's what life is all about, living and moving. You have no choice. I hate when I ask someone what did you do over the weekend and they respond, "nothing". That's impossible. You are always doing something even if you are sitting down staring at the wall. Your brain is thinking, your heart is pumping blood, your bones are holding your body up, your lungs are breathing, your skin is protecting you, and I can go on and on.

Now there is a difference between living and being alive. I heard that on a Blessed Union of Soul album. The Lord is life and we need to be urgent to find Him, as we talked about in the last few chapters. It's clear that Jesus wants us to live a new life. He tells us we must be born again. (John 3:5) He tells us that we are a new creation. (2 Corinthians 5:17) And how can we be born again at an old age? It's the Spirit, the faith, the understanding, the confession, the repentance, the baptism and Jesus' Blood. We are buried with Christ and we are born again when we come out of the waters of baptism. (Romans 6:1-8)

Now as long as we are alive the world considers us to be living but God wants us to live life to the full. (John 10:10) If we love we have passed from death to life. (1John3:14) Our physical bodies can be alive but our spiritual bodies can be dead. Jesus gave His life so we could have ours. It is so cool to love and have life. When I was writing this chapter I had come from a party of a sister celebrating her 21st birthday. She was a young Christian and she shared how she always imagined that her 21st birthday party would be so different, but she was so grateful she could spend it sober with no regrets. She came from death to life.

This chapter reminds me of one of the Matrix movies. There are many spiritual references to be made from this movie as well as a lot of concepts you can connect to Christianity. I am reminded of a particular scene in the movie when Neo enters a busy side walk with Morpheus. They are walking and talking while everyone else seems to be moving mindlessly in one direction. A similar scene is evident in the middle of Manhattan's morning rush hour.

Whenever I ride on the trains I look at people and wonder what their purpose is or if they even think about their purpose. The Purpose Driven Life by Rick Warren is a great book. I think it was a bestseller because people want a purpose, but I also think that most people are too lazy to make the choice to live on purpose. It is easier to just go with the flow. The world would be a radically different place if people understood God's purpose for their life.

We cannot continue to be conformed to the pattern of this world, we need be transformed. (Romans 12: 2) You make the decision to conform or be transformed. One of the youth camps at church was titled "Be Transformed." We want our kids to make this decision but some adults don't choose to be transformed. I have two simple thoughts on the next page to see which life you want to choose.

CONFORMED VS TRANSFORMED

Which way will you be formed? CON or SNART(trans spelled backward)
C-Coward, afraid to speak up
O-Occupied, you are too B.U.S.Y. Bound Under Satan's Yoke
N-Nobody, you are like everyone else, if you left no one would miss you
    Or
S-Special, You are God's Masterpiece, no one can replace you
N-Necessary, you are needed, you have a purpose in this world
A-Accepted, God has adopted you as His, you don't have to doubt yourself
R-Radical, one who advocates a revolution of a godly change in our society
T-Transcend, to rise above, surpass the standard and norm of the world

    We are here to make a difference. God calls us to be Holy. That means set apart. We need to transform our minds, heart, souls, strength, and whole being. We no longer need to conform to this world. The word conform means to be in agreement with. The word Con means to be against. If you choose to be a con you are going against God and you are conforming to Satan. Be smart, choose SNART. That was pretty corny, but I hope you get the point.

    They say that youth is wasted on the young and that is true in so many ways. Most people decide to become a Christian when they are older and more cautious. David slew Goliath when he was 12 years old. If more twelve year olds had a godly perspective like David we would be slaying a lot more giants in this world. Many older people don't take risks anymore and use the excuse of wisdom. We need to stop trying to change around spiritual principles and conforming them to the world's thoughts. David wasn't a loose cannon. He was faithful, and that's what we need in our churches today; the righteous who will live be faith. (Habakkuk 2:4)

    Hopefully you are encouraged to live your life the way God designed it for you. God designed you differently from me. Take your time to be transformed by God's discipline like a piece of coal being transformed by pressure and heat into a diamond. On the other hand don't waste time and delay the good you know you ought to do right now. Live your life God speed. Live your life like you are alive for the very first time. Renew your strength and fly on the wings of eagles.

    1 John 5:12 says if we have Jesus we have life and if we don't have Jesus we don't have life. Bottom line, it's that simple. If you truly get Jesus you are living the life any man or woman could ever dream of. If you don't understand Jesus then your life will always be a little bit off, you will never live the life you were created and designed to live. The journey is to fully understand Jesus and get closer and closer to Him. Hopefully as we continue on this journey together we will become more like Jesus, and draw closer to God every day. If we are doing this our lives will get better day by day. Live your life and keep drawing closer and closer to the SON!

    I realize we are on page 33 and I remember that Jesus died at age 33. As I approach 30 years old, I wonder if I only had 3 years left to my life. Would I have lived my life to the fullest potential? I am encouraged to make the most of my life. I hope you Live your Life for Jesus too.

Are you living the life you have always dreamed of?

How do you want to live your life?

What do you want your legacy to be?

1. **1 Peter 2:2-3-** Like new born babies crave milk we need to crave spiritual milk. We need to be built up and started eating some hearty meals. We have seen that the Lord is good.

2. **Deuteronomy 30:19-20-** The Lord is life. If we live a true life with Jesus as Lord we will experience life to the full.

3. **Acts 8: 26-40-** We need to be urgent. If you have not been baptized, you need to ask like Ethiopian, "What is stopping me from getting baptized?"

4. **John 8: 31- 32-** Hold to the truth. The truth will set you free so don't let it go.

5. **John 14:6-** Jesus is the way, the truth, and the life. There is only one way, one truth, and one life if we want to get to the Father.

6. **1 Peter 3: 18- 22-** Baptism saves. Please don't argue with it. It is in God's word it is not a symbol or a ceremony it is what God calls us to do. Don't make it more complicated than it is.

7. **John 3: 3-** Be born again or you cannot enter God's Kingdom. We can make that decision as an adult. No one else could make the decision for us.

Pray: That you will live a transformed life.

REST

"I'm Pleased"

Genesis 2:2-3 By the seventh Day God had finished the work he had been doing; so on the seventh day he rested from all his work. And God blessed the seventh day and made it HOLY...

With arms wide open we stand in awe
God gives good gifts and He gives us much more
He gave me the mountains and gave me the seas
He gave me the skies and all of the trees
God is amazing He gives us our rest
Searching in vain this life is the best
Couldn't imagine of asking for more
On the wings of eagles He allows me to soar
What did I do to deserve all this joy
I am no longer a man I went back to a boy

Wow, today was cool, working on rest. I usually don't get a chance to rest on Sundays but today was great. I'm actually in bed right now writing this. I listened to a great sermon today on the heart, so I'm feeling pretty good right now about having this down time. It is very easy for me to be legalistic, and to try to work my way into heaven but God gives us all a day off.

What does that mean? This can be a very touchy subject for some people. There are historical studies about this topic of the Sabbath as well as varying views on the specific day we must rest, which I do not plan to delve on in this book. I will simply share my personal convictions about the importance of rest as I see it in the scriptures, and remember that God is more concerned about the heart, not the outward appearances/actions.

Number 1 There needs to be a day where we just sit back and worship GOD. Yeah, that should be every day but it's not for most of us. It is so easy to get distracted, because there are so many things to do. That's why I believe God had to set aside one day and make it Holy. Again that does not mean you sin all of the other days except for the holy day and it doesn't mean you lock yourself in the house once a week either.

The Old Testament says keep the Sabbath day Holy. Many people still try to abide by that law. Some won't drive a car on that day, some won't cook, and some won't turn on a light switch, because all of those things are considered work to them. When Jesus healed someone on the Sabbath the Jewish leaders were angry because He did work on a day of rest. Who was wrong, Jesus or the Pharisees? I think the answer is obvious. So God doesn't say do nothing on the Sabbath. He says keep it Holy. For some people this is an excuse to be lazy. Watching TV all day and killing your brain cells does not equal up to a Sabbath's day of rest.

You do have to understand a little bit of history to figure this thing out. Back in the day people were hard workers. Jobs were strenuous and tiring. People didn't sit in front of computers all day and the factory workers didn't have these big machines where you push one button every five minutes. Work was Work. So people were truly tired, and they couldn't just text message someone to see how they were doing, they had to check up on the person physically. To get to wherever they were going they couldn't just hop in their car and drive five miles or jump on the train for 15 stops. It was work to get to have fellowship.

So to give people a break, God said make one day Holy. Rest. Perhaps, the Sabbath day was originally a Saturday and that some and for historical reasons church services were changed to Sunday but it doesn't makes a difference. Going to church on Sunday does not equate keeping the Sabbath day and having a day of rest. Many of us attend a variety of church related meetings throughout the week, and most Sundays feel like a work day because of all we are trying to accomplish during and after services.

Therefore, for most of us, with a conventional work schedule, our rest should be on a Saturday. You should take a good chunk of time on Saturdays to spend time with just you and God. Pray, give thanks, sing

36

songs of praise, write a letter of confession, and study the Scriptures deeply. Can you help someone move? Maybe, just don't let it consume your whole day. Can you share your faith on the streets or in a mall? Of course, that brings refreshing. Can you email people encouraging letters, can you drive to the mountains, can you watch an inspirational movie? Can you listen to uplifting music? Will it bring you closer to God? Will it be revitalizing, spiritual? Will it be Holy? Then do it, and enjoy your time of rest.

Let's look at four scriptures that teach us about that Sabbath. First, in Matthew 12:1-8 Jesus was in the field with His disciples on the Sabbath. They were hungry so they picked some grain to eat. The Pharisees looked at them and judged them. Jesus immediately went back to the Scriptures and gave them two examples of why what they were doing was fine. They were hungry so they ate on the Sabbath. What do you think? Jesus ends up by saying He is Lord of the Sabbath. What does that mean for us today?

In Luke 13:10-17 Jesus taught on the Sabbath. While He was teaching, a crippled woman came in. So Jesus did what He always does. He healed her. And again the Pharisees had a problem with that. They did not want Jesus to eat and now they don't want Him to heal. So Jesus was indignant again. He called them hypocrites. The Pharisees would help their animals if they were in need but they had a problem with helping a human. Weird thinking!?!

Then in Exodus 20:8-11 God tells us to remember the Sabbath. It is one of the Ten Commandments. It also has the longest explanations of all the other commandments. God goes into the detail of how this reflects the six days that God worked. He also says one day out of the seven will be Holy because one of those days God rested. So even though we see Jesus eating and healing on the Sabbath that does not take away that this is a Holy day.

The last thought comes from Hebrews 4:1-11. It starts off by saying that the promises of still entering His rest remains. In verse two it goes on to explain that to enter the rest we have to combine it with faith and if we believe we will enter. If we do not have faith and harden our hearts we will not enter His rest. So we can tell by this passage that it still mentions to take a rest from our work, but moreover it is telling us that we need to enter God's eternal rest. So, if we are disobedient we will miss out on that opportunity.

This Sabbath conversation can get a little bit tricky, but like everything else God does, it really is not confusing. He wants us to act in faith. The rest is for us to connect with Him. Can we eat during the rest? Can we help someone? Of course! But the rest is for us, so we can be revitalized. So we can work harder and more diligently the rest of the week. Bottom line, we will never be completely rested until we ultimately see God face to face and enter His eternal rest. So make some time to rest with God, Worship Him, Enjoy Him and He will fill you up.

How do you feel about rest?

Are you lazy or are you a workaholic?

Why do you think God put the Sabbath day in the 10 commandments?

1. **Ephesians 1: 3-12-** Even though we have the adult decision to choose Jesus, God still chose us and we always have to stop and remember that.

2. **2 Thessalonians 3:16-** The Lord of peace will give you peace. He is the only one who can give you true peace.

3. **Habakkuk 3:2-5-** I stand in awe to see what you have done for me. When we keep moving and working we can lose sight and start to be deceived and believe that we are working more than God.

4. **Hebrews 3:16-19-** We can enter God's rest if we have not hardened out hearts but we believe His word.

5. **Matthew 11:28-30-** He provides rest for the weary. If you are really working for the Lord you should be tired. But He will be the one to comfort you.

6. **Exodus 31:14-17-** Observe the Sabbath it is Holy. It is in the 10 commandments for a reason.

7. **Colossians 2:16-17-** Don't be deceived by the New moon or Sabbath dates. Don't let people make you feel guilty with their traditions. Jesus is the real deal.

Pray: That you can sit back and appreciate God's Love.

Stop

Jesus is Lord

The Cost of Being a Disciple: Luke 14: 25-35

Large crowds were traveling with Jesus, and turning to them he said: If anyone comes to me and does not hate his father and mother, his wife and children, his brothers and sisters—yes, even his own life—he cannot be my disciple. And anyone who does not carry his cross and follow me cannot be my disciple.

Suppose one of you wants to build a tower. Will he not first sit down and estimate the cost to see if he has enough money to complete it? For if he lays the foundation and is not able to finish it, everyone who sees it will ridicule him, saying, 'This fellow began to build and was not able to finish.

Or suppose a king is about to go to war against another king. Will he not first sit down and consider whether he is able with ten thousand men to oppose the one coming against him with twenty thousand? If he is not able, he will send a delegation while the other is still a long way off and will ask for terms of peace. In the same way, any of you who does not give up everything he has cannot be my disciple!

First things first: God, Jesus, The Holy Spirit, and Christianity, are not add-ons to a nice life you already had. If you understand and accept the teachings of the Bible you are a whole new creation when you decide to make Jesus Lord of your life. You have to stop your old way of living, way of thinking, and way of being. We do not add Jesus to our lives; Jesus has to become our lives. We need to stop everything we were doing and become like little children and learn to live and love again.

Anyone who came to Jesus was usually surprised by the answers He gave to them when they asked to follow Him. Stuff like *"go and sell everything you own"*, *"Deny your self"*, *"Hate your family"*, *"Hate your self"*. People don't want to accept these challenges, but the expectations are still true today. The Bible doesn't change and God's plans make sense.

Even if you were a pastor at another church, who didn't get the true gospel, you are a new creation. It's tough because you might have some good knowledge already but you have to wipe your mind clean so it could be filled with the truth from the Holy Spirit. It's a scary thought, that's why God says we have to count to cost.

Sometimes the people who get the gospel the most are the ones with the most issues. The ones who were forgiven most love the most. (Luke 7:47) Some of us come with our old traditions and thoughts. We can say *when I grew up this is not how we did things*. God does not care about any of that. It is not about your traditions or what you are used to. It's God's way or the highway. So just face it and give up, God wins.

I have been watching American Gladiators again. There is a guy named Justice on the show and he is a big dude. It is funny to hear people talk trash to the Gladiators and get demolished. Most people have no chance against Justice, but God is way bigger than a gladiator, so none of us have a chance when we go up against God. We do not want God's justice, we just need His mercy.

I'm sure you have heard the song, "Stop in the Name of Love". The next line goes, "before you break my heart, think it o-o-ver." I think God is singing those lines to you. He wants you to stop in the name of Love. That's who God is. He is love. He tells us to stop because it is good for us. If we don't stop it will break His heart, so we need to think it over.

There is another song that reminds me of this topic, maybe not as popular. Digital Underground sings "Stop what you're doin' cause I'm about to ruin the image and the style that ya used to." That is another thing that God does. He ruins the image and the style that we are used to. Being a Christian should be something totally new. You should feel like you are getting brainwashed because your brain needs to be washed from all the dirt that was in it.

Let me make this VERY clear, there are some cults out there that do want to brainwash you in the wrong way. God is the only one who should wash your brain. Never, ever, in NO Way should you do what a man tells you to do. You need to be motivated by Jesus your Lord and His word only. Do not be swayed by men. They might have some good things to say, but you must always go back to God. God does the work in us. Let's trust in Him.

It is a scary thing when people trust men more than they trust God. So many people don't go to church because they don't trust organized religion; they don't trust as a result of the hypocrisy they see in people. Although there are many churches out there that are deceived and deceiving people, there are also churches out there that are doing a good job of sharing God's truth. We will talk more about this later.

Let's also understand that we are saved by grace. It is not what we do that makes us saved. Grace is free gift. The New Geneva Study Bible says, in its notes for Galatians 1:3, "Grace" translates the Greek charis, which means 'an undeserved act of kindness'. Paul uses this word more often than any other New Testament writer and gives it immense theological significance. It refers to all that God has given us in Christ; nothing of which we have earned or can repay."

So we need to have faith in this grace, understanding that faith and deeds work together. What is it to live by faith? The book of Hebrews tells us without faith it is impossible to please God, and we are here to please God, to be obedient children. Faith is being certain of what we hope for. We need to believe that God will save us.

Philippians 1:6 tells us, being confident of this, that He who began a good work in you will carry it on to completion until the day of Christ Jesus, and Romans 3:24 tells us we are justified freely by His grace through the redemption that came by Christ Jesus.

We must do as Philippians 3:7-9 and consider everything a loss compared to Christ. Galatians 5:11 tells the brothers, if I am still preaching circumcision, why am I still being persecuted? In that case the offense of the cross has been abolished. It is not the things that we do, it is all about Christ. And that is why we do things because Christ has done it all. Let's look at three practical examples of discipleship:

First Mark 1:16-20 tells us our response needs to be urgent. Once we realize God's grace the response should be immediate. This decision happens every time you have a choice to follow Jesus. We need to choose Him quickly

Second Luke 9: 57- 62 tells us that once we understand Jesus, He must come first in our lives. There can be no other excuses or no other distractions. There are many things we will have to do in life and Jesus still has to come first in every move.

Lastly, in Luke 14: 25-35 we are told to count the cost, which is the scripture at the beginning of the chapter. We need to make sure we love God before our wife, children, and even our own life and if we can't say that, then Jesus is not Lord. And that is the only thing that counts. Our good confession is that Jesus is Lord. Jesus must rule our thoughts actions and attitudes. I hope you will make the right decision daily to STOP and surrender all to Jesus. If He is our King then we will be part of His Kingdom.

What old habits do you still have?

What steps do you need to take to stop your bad habits?

How often do you need to remind yourself that you are a new creation?

1. Matt 9:16, Mark 2:21, Luke 5:36- Tell us about the new cloth. We have to put on a whole new outfit. We cannot just was the old clothes we have.

2. Mark 10: 17-29- Jesus calls us to leave everything, but He also says He will give us more in return. The rich young man did not understand what Jesus was teaching him.

3. 2 Timothy 2:8- Jesus was raised from the dead, so He wants us to be raised from the dead also.

4. Matthew 13: 44-46- This man gave up every thing for the thing of value. If we find some thing that makes sense we have to drop the old stuff that does not make sense anymore.

5. Matthew 22: 36-39- 'Love the Lord your God with all your heart and with all your soul and with your entire mind.'

6. 2 Corinthians 5: 14-17- We are a new creation. The old is gone. We need to act in that way.

7. Matt 9: 17, Mark 2: 22, Luke 5: 37- 38- All talk about new wine skins. It is a continuation from the first 3 verses. Jesus wants us to under stand that we need to be something totally new.

Pray: That you will commit that Jesus is Lord today and everyday.

42

Step 9

Drop

You got to Pray just to make it today

This, then, is how you should pray:
" 'Our Father in heaven,
hallowed be your name,
your kingdom come,
your will be done
on earth as it is in heaven.
Give us today our daily bread.
Forgive us our debts,
as we also have forgiven our debtors.
And lead us not into temptation,
but deliver us from the evil one. (NIV)
Our Father in heaven,
Reveal who you are. Set the world right;
Do what's best— as above, so below.
Keep us alive with three square meals.
Keep us forgiven with you and forgiving others.
Keep us safe from ourselves and the Devil.
You're in charge!
You can do anything you want!
You're ablaze in beauty!
Yes. Yes. Yes(The Message)
Our Father which art in heaven, Hallowed be thy name. Thy
kingdom come, Thy will be done in earth, as it is in heaven.
Give us this day our daily bread. And forgive us our debts, as
we forgive our debtors. And lead us not into temptation, but
deliver us from evil: For thine is the kingdom, and the power,
and the glory, for ever. Amen. (King James Version)
Matthew 6:9-13

How long do you pray for in a day? How much is ten minutes of your time worth? Could you drop right now and do 10 push-ups? Could you drop on your knees and pray for ten specific things?

This chapter is about prayer, not a made-up prayer but a genuine prayer. Prayer is one of the most powerful things you can do. Prayer can drive out demons. (Mark 9:26-29) Did you ever pray through the Psalms to see how David prayed? David was real in prayer as he worshiped God. Let us learn how to make our prayers more in depth than David.

Since Jesus stops us from falling because He gives us the right path to travel we need to fall for Jesus and drop on our knees. He wants us to bow down and worship Him. If we don't pray we will fall away. Though we are freed from sin we choose to become a slave to God. Since slavery has negative connotations people tend to look at God like a slave driver with a list of rules, the truth is we simply are making a commitment to a God who is our best friend and we actually receive true freedom.

Try giving it all to Jesus. Let go and let God. That's why people are so stressed out, we try and do everything ourselves. I realize I am messed up so it makes sense for me to lay down my life and give it to the One who created the universe. I am confident that He is able to handle my life. We all need to start off with a trusting attitude that God can do it.

James 5:16 tells us that the prayer of a righteous man is powerful and effective. So number one, that means we have to train our selves to be righteous if we want to have powerful and effective prayers. There are people who just throw out little prayers in times of distress and God answers, but don't get envious of them and use that as your standard. You need to train yourself to be a prayer warrior. The disciple James was called old camel knees, because he spent so much time on his knees praying. I want to use people like that to be my example of prayer.

It is also very good to pray with others for that reason. Sometimes we get in a slump and don't know what to pray for. It is good to hear what is on others' hearts. I love praying with my buddy Kevin Finnerty, he is so specific when he prays. He remembers people who are sick. He prays for the leaders of our nation. He prays through specific homework assignments of his daughters. He prays for people who are studying the Bible. He prays for people in his Bible talk. The list goes on, and that example helps me to deepen my prayer life.

There is a lot on our minds and a lot on our plates. We need to learn how to pray it out. Many of us don't even know how to talk it out. Both are learning experiences. Most things you learn by someone's example. The disciples ask Jesus, "teach us to pray." On the title page of this chapter I have the Lord's Prayer written out in three different translations. That is the prayer that Jesus used to teach the disciples how to pray, along with all of the other prayers that He modeled on a daily basis, as seen throughout the New Testament. Let's break this prayer down a little further.

Father ...God, Abba, Lord, Call His Name when you start off in Prayer. A prayer is different from thinking; you are talking to God.

Hallowed be your name, --- God is Holy, to mention His name should be set apart, like in the movie The Lion King, when the name Mufasa was spoken the hyenas shivered.

Your Kingdom Come. --- Your kingdom is here, your kingdom is coming. It is a paradox but we pray for His kingdom on earth and we pray for His kingdom in heaven.

Give us each day our daily bread --- Give me what I need every day. We have a lot more wants than needs.

Forgive us our sins --- Ask for forgiveness because you always sin, God forgives us regardless but asking for forgiveness keeps us humble.

For we also forgive everyone who sins against us --- I love how this comes next. We need to forgive if we want forgiveness. When we ask for forgiveness we also need to have repentance backing it up.

And lead us not into temptation --- protect us from Satan's schemes. We are weak but God makes us strong.

If you just work on your prayer life you will get better at it. Jesus gave us a guideline because we need it. Like any form of communication we can always improve it. The ACTS prayer is another practical that is always a good guide for me. I don't remember where it came from. I was taught it and used it since I was a young Christian.

A-Admire Philippians 4: 8 tells us to think about things that are admirable. What is admirable about God? I have also used the word adoration. What do you adore about God? This is a time to praise Him, a time to acknowledge how great He is. He works miracles in your life. He sustains your life every day. He provides your every need. I think those things along with many others are worthy or respect.

C-Confession Nehemiah 9: 2-3 says that the people spent six hours confessing sin. That's a lot of confession. I know I am guilty many a time of going through prayers without confession. I also know that every day I struggle with sin. No, I don't murder someone every day or I do not commit adultery. But I do struggle with thoughts of hate and lust. Jesus tells us that the thoughts are just as bad. Stay humble and confess.

T-Thanks 1 Thessalonians 5: 18 says give thanks in all circumstances. This is a little bit easier for me. 99% of the time I start off my prayers by giving thanks to God. One thing I understand is that life is not guaranteed. I also understand that my life is much better than many other people in the world. I have a huge list to be thankful for. Even when it does not seem that way there is still a lot to give thanks for.

S-Supplication 1 Kings 8: 54 King Solomon offered prayers and supplications up to the Lord. Supplication is just a fancy word for what you want. This is that last part because this is the easiest. We all know how to ask for things. I don't need to add much for this one.

I hope this helps and you get some time right now to drop to your knees and pray.

How often do you pray?

How can you add more quantity to your prayer?

How can you add more quality to your prayer?

1. **Luke 11:1-13-** The disciples ask Jesus to teach them how to pray. He gives them the Lord's Prayer. He continues on by telling them to keep asking God for things and He is the on that provides.

2. **Luke 18:1-8-** Jesus wants us to be like the persistent widow. We will not annoy God when we are asking Him to bless us. He loves us.

3. **Luke 18:9-14-** Jesus uses the Pharisee and tax collector as examples of what is right and wrong about prayers. Basically be Humble when you pray. It is not a time to show off, God already knows your heart.

4. **Psalm 17:1-** Hear, O LORD, my righteous plea; listen to my cry. Give ear to my prayer. We need to be totally open and honest when we pray.

5. **Daniel 9:4-** We need to praise God when we pray and give Him the utmost respect.

6. **Matthew 6:7** - Don't babble when you pray. When you add a lot of words it doesn't make the prayers any better. It actually makes it less sincere.

7. **Matthew 21:22-** If you believe, you will receive whatever you ask for in prayer. That is a pretty cool promise.

Pray: Just Pray.

Role

WWJD

Amazing
Blameless
Committed
Dedicated, Devoted
Empowering, Energetic
Friendly, Forceful, Faithful
Godly, Gracious, Great
Humble, Holy, Helpful,
Intelligent, Important
Just, Joyful,
Kind,
Loving,
Merciful,
Noticeable,
Outstanding
Peaceful, Patient
Quiet, Qualified
Radical, Real, Reliable
Sacrificial, Servant, Self-controlled
Trustworthy, Truthful
Understanding
Victorious
Wise
Zealous

Jesus   You

Compare yourself to Jesus from A-Z

Jesus needs to be our role model. Do you remember those corny wrist bands that came out a while ago that said WWJD. It stood for what would Jesus do? I'm sure you've seen them. I'm sure they are still in circulation now. (Such a dorky fashion statement, but what a profound message) Imagine if before we made any move we asked ourselves that question and responded in the proper manner.

That is exactly what we need to do. We need to do what He did. He got baptized, He prayed, He came to seek and save the lost, and many other things that the Bible tells us. Paul says follow me as I follow Christ. (1 Corinthians 11:1) We need to be that example, too. When Christ is our role model and we use Him as an example for how to live our lives, then we can be a role model to others.

Jesus was a perfect model of perfect love (1 John 4). That is His greatest example for us to follow. He wraps up in the book of John by saying how much He loves us and encouraging us to lay down our lives for one another. He was the word in the flesh. He was God as a man, but everything He did was perfect. It is amazing.

I've been told that I look like the "typical" Jesus image when I grow my hair and my beard. So I have played the role of Jesus in some performances at church. When I get the opportunities to act out Jesus it proves to be the best times for me spiritually because it forces me to study out what Jesus did and why He did it. One of the most challenging scenes to act out was Jesus with the woman caught in adultery. What was Jesus thinking? She was caught in the act of adultery. What was she wearing? What did He write in the sand? We need to study out Jesus in every situation in order to connect to Him, and imitate Him.

Jesus is real. He is not a fictional character. He is in the history books. He was tempted in every way but did not sin, so we can't say that He can not relate. He went through everything, and modeled who we need to be in each circumstance. He could not be the pansy Jesus that most of us see pictures of. Jesus flipped over tables, He confronted leaders and told them they were hypocrites, and He told his friends that they were acting like Satan. He spoke the truth. He didn't back down. He was a man's man. He was compassionate, He wept, He loved children, He took care of His mom, He knew how to speak to women, and He was in touch with His sensitive side.

It is hard to find a good role model these days, especially for men. What does a real man look like today? Most kids have no idea. We need to give them the perfect picture through the Bible. Manhood in the 21st Century has become despicable and deplorable. Even when we think we can use someone as a role model they do something crazy. The Yankees give A-Rod millions of dollars then we find out he was using steroids and fooling around behind his wife's back. Michael Phelps is hailed as one of the greatest athletes of all times then he goes and celebrates with marijuana. Chris Brown is every girl's dream boyfriend then we find out he beat his girlfriend Rihanna right before the EMMY awards. I pray for these guys, but right now they are not setting a godly example.

Let's look at who Jesus was through the Scriptures. These are just a few that shows what type of character He had from A-Z.

Approachable: Matthew 17:14 a man approached Jesus and knelt before Him.
Bold: Matthew 23:33 "You snakes! You brood of vipers! How will you escape being condemned to hell?"
Compassionate: Matthew 9:36 He had compassion on them.
Decisive: Luke 13:32 "Go tell that fox, 'I will drive out demons and heal people today and tomorrow, and on the third day I will reach my goal.'"
Empowering: John 15:5 "I am the vine; you are the branches."
Friendly: Matthew 26:50 "Friend, do what you came for."
Godly: Matthew 16:16 "You are the Christ, the Son of the living God."
Humble: Matthew 11:29 I am gentle and humble in heart
Intelligent: Matthew 22:18 But Jesus, knowing their evil intent,
Just: 1 Corinthians 6:11 You were justified in the name of the Lord Jesus Christ
Kind: Ephesians 2:7 Expressed in His kindness to us in Christ Jesus.
Loving: John 15:9 "As the Father has loved me, so have I loved you."
Merciful: Matthew 9:13 "I desire mercy, not sacrifice."
Noticeable: Mark 6:14 Jesus' name had become well known.
Outstanding: Mark 7:37 People were overwhelmed with amazement. "He has done everything well."
Peaceful: Romans 5:1 we have peace with God through our Lord Jesus Christ
Quiet: Mark 14:61 But Jesus remained silent
Radical: Matthew 18:9 "And if your eye causes you to sin, gouge it out."
Sacrificial: 1 John 2:2 He is the atoning sacrifice for our sins.
Trustworthy: John 14:1 "Trust in God; trust also in me."
Understanding: Luke 2:47 Everyone who heard Him was amazed at his understanding and his answers.
Victorious: 1 Corinthians 15:57 Victory through our Lord Jesus Christ.
Wise: Matthew 13:54 "Where did this man get this wisdom?"
Zealous: John 2:17 it is written: "Zeal for your house will consume me."

Matthew 22:16 "Teacher," they said, "we know you are a man of integrity and that you teach the way of God in accordance with the truth. You aren't swayed by men, because you pay no attention to who they are."
Thank You, Jesus, for still being the perfect role model.

Hopefully we will also become men and women who will become the role models of today. We need to continue to seek out practical wisdom. There are many books out there that give us some practical examples. Like a Tree Planted by a Stream by G. Steve Kinnard, The Power of Spiritual Thinking by Gordon Ferguson. Those titles are published by *ipi* and *dpi* which provide many titles for practical Christian living.

How did you compare to Jesus on the first page?

What changes can you make today to be more like Jesus?

What character issues do you need to pray about to be more like Jesus?

1. **Luke 11:39-52-** Jesus rebukes the Pharisees because He does not just desire for us to follow a bunch of rules. When we do not get it from the heart Jesus says, WOE!

2. **John 2:15-19-** Jesus clears the temple because He was serious about righteousness. He did not just sit back. Jesus got up and did some thing.

3. **John 4:7-10-** Jesus talked with the Samaritan woman. He was different. He did not care about status.

4. **Matthew 5:48-** Be perfect. That's a pretty high calling. So we can't stop striving. We will always have more to work on.

5. **Matthew 5:17-20-** Jesus came to fulfill the law. So we need to be better than the Pharisees.

6. **Matthew 28:18 −20-** All authority has been given to Jesus. So what ever He says goes.

7. **John 15:12-17-** Jesus calls us friends. He tells us His business. We have a big part in Jesus' life. I hope that makes you feel encouraged.

Pray: That God will change you to be more like Jesus.

Say no
SIN

A young boy named Francois from the Ivory Coast in West Africa was offered a job in a cocoa plantation one summer. Work was not easy to come by in his region of Africa so he accepted the job immediately. The plantation was so big and beautiful it reminded him of the Garden of Eden. There were many fruits available to him at will even including cola nuts. Sucking on the cola nuts had a similar effect to that from a strong cup of espresso. It almost seemed like he was getting paid to have fun.

But it did get hot on the plantation and it was a long walk back to the well to draw water. However, there was area where an outcropping of rocks would catch some rain water and create puddles. Francois noticed other boys drinking from the stagnant water but he was too afraid to try it for himself. One day he rationalized to himself if everyone else is doing it can't be that bad. He soon learned that was the stupidest mistake he ever made.

As little Francois drank the stagnant water, he had no idea he was turning his life into a living nightmare. Francois had ingested a parasite which was living in the stagnant water called the Guinea Worm. At first something like pimples appeared on his legs. Then they became swollen and painful and began to look like boils. The pain was excruciating and he would cry when his father would touch a sensitive area. Eventually the worm was visible just below the skin in a zigzag pattern up his leg for over two feet in length.

To get the worm out Francois' father had to puncture the abscesses formed by the worm with a red hot screw. After screaming from this eye popping experience, he looked down in amazement as the end of the worm became visible. It actually wiggled within the wound.

The only way to deal with this medical horror is to simply allow the worm to wiggle out on his own. The exposed worm is then rolled up on a matchstick as it emerges. The process is painful and lasts up to a month. Francois pulled out ten worms over the next five months.

-Paraphrased from "The Killer Within" by Mike Taliaferro

After sharing this true story Mike states, "It always amazes me how one small act can change your entire life. A simple decision can make all the difference." I agree so much with that statement and I am so convicted (and disgusted) by the story from his book. But it is so true how sin destroys our life. The Bible makes sin very clear. Galatians 5:19-21 gives us a good list to start off with. I shared it from three different versions so you could get a better idea.

(NIV) The acts of the sinful nature are obvious: sexual immorality, impurity, and debauchery; idolatry and witchcraft; hatred, discord, jealousy, fits of rage, selfish ambition, dissensions, factions and envy; drunkenness, orgies, and the like.

(King James Version) Now the works of the flesh are manifest, which are these; Adultery, fornication, uncleanness, lasciviousness, Idolatry, witchcraft, hatred, variance, emulations, wrath, strife, seditions, heresies, envyings, murders, drunkenness, reveling and such like.

(The Message) It is obvious what kind of life develops out of trying to get your own way all the time: repetitive, loveless, cheap sex; a stinking accumulation of mental and emotional garbage; frenzied and joyless grabs for happiness; trinket gods; magic-show religion; paranoid loneliness; cutthroat competition; all-consuming-yet-never-satisfied wants; a brutal temper; an impotence to love or be loved; divided homes and divided lives; small-minded and lopsided pursuits; the vicious habit of depersonalizing everyone into a rival; uncontrolled and uncontrollable addictions; ugly parodies of community.

Sin is obvious. Sometimes we deceive ourselves by saying we don't know what sin is, or ask the question is this really sin, but the Bible says it is obvious. If you are not a Christian reading this book it might not be as obvious because you are blinded by sin. Satan is a liar. He always wants it to seem like sin is not bad. God created everything good for our enjoyment but Satan tells us that we are deprived and we need more. I think this is Satan's biggest way of tempting us.

Sex is good. God created women to be pleasing to men, but the Devil wants us to believe that sex outside of marriage is the way to go. Statistics tell us why that's bad; broken homes, divorce, sexually transmitted diseases, the list of other dramas go on and on.

The Bible says eat, drink and be merry, but when we overeat we get all sorts of health problems, diabetes, high cholesterol, heart attacks, loss of energy. When we drink too much there is domestic violence, there are car accidents, and there is alcohol poisoning. When we try to be extra merry by taking drugs, we get arrested, we lose our minds, we go to rehab centers, and we have to be on all sorts of treatments for life. It's obvious.

Then all the other sins fall under the golden rule. Do unto others as you would have them do unto you. Do you want someone to steal from you, don't do it to some one else. Do you want someone to be greedy or selfish when you are in need or to be generous and giving? Do you want someone to curse you out and punch you in the face? So be kind to others. You know the list could go on forever so stop sinning. If you know the good you ought to do and you don't do it you are sinning. (James 4:16)

I hate sin. It kills; it ruins the perfect world God created. People get entangled in it for life and then they go to Hell. It is destructive, disgusting, disgraceful, deceitful, and dumb. Some of us still can't stop. Why? Romans 7:7-25 explains.

It can actually seem very mixed up when you first look at it and in a way that is true. Satan likes to throw us into confusion because that's what he does. Paul starts off by saying that the Law produced death in him. How could something good produce death? Because it showed him his fault. He said he did not recognize his faults before he knew the law. Now that he knows it, he also knows he is not living by it. I am sure we can relate. I was always taught that a "white lie" is ok, but when I read the Bible and I read that all lies are sin and all liars had a place in hell, I had to repent.

Philippians 3:18 tells us, "For, as I have often told you before and now say again even with tears, many live as enemies of the cross of Christ." That is what sin does; it makes you an enemy of the cross, the cross that Jesus suffered so much for you to give you forgiveness of sins. When you live trying to please the things that Jesus suffered and died for, you are saying you don't need God's forgiveness. I can go as far as saying you are doing the same as the ones who were actually there crucifying Christ. You are spitting on Him, slapping His face, and giving Him 40 lashes all over again.

Sin kills. It killed Jesus and it will kill you. Not only is the Bible trying to protect you from Hell but it also protects you from the everyday troubles of life. If I tell a lie I have to worry about keeping up with that lie at least and worst it could end me up in jail or even dead. Stealing sets up a horrible circle. First you don't learn how to work for things. You prove that you have no value for others and you make the economy worse because we have to compensate for bums like you. I can go on and on with the list of sins and their consequences but I hope you get the point.

My last thought is "Flee from Sin". Joseph is a great example of this in Genesis 39:6-12. If most of us were in his situation, we would have probably fallen right away. First they said he was handsome and well built. Then they said he had great responsibility. He was also far away from home and from any accountability. She was probably very good looking. What did Joseph choose to do? He ran away. Why? Because he knew it was a sin against God. He didn't know about Jesus. He didn't even have to confess to someone if he did do something wrong, but he understood that he did not want to sin against God. I pray we can bring these convictions back to men and women in God's kingdom. Sin is out to get you so run away as fast as you can. God's watching.

Which sin haunts you the most?

Why is it so hard for you to stop committing the same sins?

What do you need to do to change you mind about that sin?

1. **Romans 3:23-** We all sin. This is not in the Bible to say that it is ok to sin. It is there to show that we all need Jesus. No one is exempt.

2. **Roman 6:23-** Sin equals death. If we all sin than we all deserve death. Jesus is the only one who can save us from that.

3. **Romans 7:11-** Sin is deceptive. Romans 7 helps us to understand it. It can get confusing if we are tied up in sin. So Romans 8 tells us how the Holy Spirit helps us with that.

4. **John 8:34-** We are slave to sin. They control us. That's why we need God's Spirit to control.

5. **Psalm 69:1-5-** Sin traps us in the muck and mire. We need to cry out to God to help us out of it.

6. **Colossians 2:11-12-** Bury your sin. It is not beneficial to anyone. You are sinless with Christ. Keep it that way.

7. **James 1:12-15-** Sin gives birth to death. It starts from a desire so we need to cut it down before it gets too far.

Pray: Ask God for forgiveness of you sins, thank Him for His forgiveness.

Then Go

DO SOMETHING

Timeline, of the man who traded a paperclip for a house, based on the website and as summarized by the BBC

On July 14, 2005, he went to Vancouver and traded the paperclip for a fish-shaped pen. He then traded the pen the same day for a hand-sculpted doorknob from Seattle, Washington, which he nicknamed "Knob-T". On July 25, 2005, he traveled to Amherst, Massachusetts, with a friend to trade the Knob-T for a Coleman camp stove (with fuel). On September 24, 2005, he went to San Clemente, California, and traded the camp stove for a Honda generator, from a U.S. Marine. On November 16, 2005, he made a second (and successful) attempt (after having the generator confiscated by the New York City Fire Department) in Maspeth, Queens, to trade the generator for an "instant party": an empty keg, an IOU for filling the keg with the beer of the holder's choice, and a neon Budweiser sign. On December 8, 2005, he traded the "instant party" to Quebec comedian and radio personality Michel Barrette for a Ski-doo snowmobile. Within a week of that, he traded the snowmobile for a two-person trip to Yahk, British Columbia, in February 2006. On or about January 7, 2006, the second person on the trip to Yahk traded Kyle a cube van for the privilege. On or about February 22, 2006, he traded the cube van for a recording contract with Metal Works in Toronto, Canada. On or about April 11, 2006, he traded the recording contract to Jody Gnant for a year's rent in Phoenix, Arizona. On or about April 26, 2006, he traded the one year's rent in Phoenix, Arizona, for one afternoon with Alice Cooper On or about May 26, 2006, he traded the one afternoon with Alice Cooper for a KISS motorized snow globe On or about June 2, 2006, he traded the KISS motorized snow globe to Corbin Bernsen for a role in the film Donna on Demand.[9] On or about July 5, 2006, he traded the movie role for a two-story farmhouse in Kipling, Saskatchewan

That is a funny story but we can see that he made something out of nothing or a paperclip if you want to get technical. God also calls us to do something. We need a good defense but we need a good offense also.

James 4:7-10 tells us to resist the devil, that is Step 11, and he will flee from you and when you draw near to God, He will draw near to you. The goal is not just to resist. The goal is to be purified. Satan throws garbage at us all day. He sets up his angels to attack us in the craftiest ways. Even if we resist all of his junk we are bound to get a little soiled on our clothes. We need to go to God and clean up. But the fight is going on right now so let's talk about our game plan.

Our first weapon against Satan is prayer; praying for protection and praying to keep our hearts pure. It is so cool how God created animals with all of their defense mechanisms. I got a puffer fish from the Dominican Republic. It has spikes that puff up on its body when it is under attack. There are so many other animals and plants that have other unique defense systems. I believe they set an example for us because we need to be on the defense against Satan.

Ephesians 6:10-17 tells us how to boost our defense against sin. We have to put on our armor of God and each part has its purpose. The belt of truth - you can't lie so you speak the truth. When you speak the truth you know you can stand firm because you have nothing to hide. Next is the breast plate of righteousness - you guard your heart when you do what's right. If your heart is filled and protected by righteous things you make it difficult for sin to creep in. Then there are feet fitted for readiness - that comes from the Gospel, we can go and share the word of God. We first share it with our selves then we can share it with others. The shield of faith is next - If you believe, you can extinguish the arrows from Satan. Remember, Satan is a liar. You have to know and believe the truth. Then the Helmet of salvation - It protects your mind to know that God saved you. A mind is a terrible thing to waste. Don't lose your minds to sinful thoughts. Finally, the sword of the Holy Spirit- Whatever else is left over the Holy Spirit will help you destroy it. There are many different parts of the Armor of God because Satan has many different schemes.

God wants to prepare us for all of them. You can't just say no to the lie, you've have to replace it with the truth. For example, you can't just stare at that chocolate cake and say, *I'm not going to eat, I'm not going to eat.* First of all that is lust, second you are worthless at that moment because you are frozen by your evil desires, and third you more than likely will eventually fall into the temptation and eat that cake. You have to replace it. A healthy snack like an apple can be an option.

I'm not just talking about eating healthy snacks. In most situations we can't just exchange, we have to do something totally different. You can't say, *Oh, there is a struggling video on BET let me turn it to MTV to see another struggling video.* You have to do something totally different. Like Joseph ran away from Potiphar's wife as we mentioned in the previous chapter. I'm sure he would have had some momentary pleasures but he saw the later consequences. We need to run. Maybe run means get out of the house and pray, read a book, make a phone call, go work out, share you faith; do something, don't just stand there.

Sometimes it's just the little things we do that help the most. I know some people get stuck by the "paralysis of analysis." They think so much about what they want to do, they don't do anything. Some people just think about doing something so big, like converting the whole neighborhood, baptizing everyone who won a Grammy award, studying the Bible with Barack Obama and Hillary Clinton together, ending the war, solving the world hunger crisis, finding a cure for every disease. Now those are great things, but those are not things that happen overnight, and they are not things that are single handedly done. Most of the times God just wants you to do the simple things like: invite someone to a Bible discussion, serve in the children's ministry, ask someone how they are doing, share how your sin got you in trouble, share how God has changed your life. God is interested in individual souls. One at a time. Strive for the great things. But don't just sit there and think about it.

God made you, YOU. If you think you are not strong enough, smart enough, rich enough, pretty enough, or anything else you can think of, you are wrong. And don't say not *yet, when I move, when this situation changes, I don't have enough knowledge of the Bible,* again those are all lies from Satan. Time doesn't stop and Satan doesn't stop, so we have to keep on keeping on.

But you are not strong enough on your own. Many men of the Bible sinned because they did not replace there temptation. David was a man after God's own heart and when he was idle he committed adultery. His son Solomon was the wisest man but he could not figure out how to tame his desire for women. Samson was the strongest dude but he couldn't fight off a little woman. When we are not actively fighting off sin Satan will attack us and we will fall.

You say you don't know what to do? I'll give you a list of 10 things to do:
1. Read this book or another spiritual book, even better read the Bible
2. Go outside on a prayer walk, regardless of the weather
3. Share your faith when you go for the walk, talk about your life
4. Go serve someone, clean their house, cook them dinner, baby-sit
5. Make a phone call, call a family member, call a Christian, call a friend
6. Go work out, go to gym, ride your bike, go jogging, do push-ups
7. Clean your house, tidy up a room that you have been neglecting
8. Write a sermon, prepare a communion message or a study on sin
9. Go visit an old friend or family member you have not seen for a while
10. Continue working on your story, your struggles and victories

I'm sure you can come up with more things than these. I just give these as an example for when you say you are bored and there is nothing to do. We do not fall into sin. We deliberately choose to sin, so we have to deliberately choose not to sin. It's all to your benefit to go and do something great for God.

What do you do to replace sin?

When are the times you are most likely to sin?

What activity can you replace in that time?

1. **Luke 21:1-4-** The widow's offering was small, but she gave something and she gave with a big heart.

2. **2 Corinthians 5:19-** We make it our goal to please Him. We need to have a goal if we want to accomplish something.

3. **James 2:14-18-** We need to have faith and deeds as James tells us. The book of James has a lot of practical lessons.

4. **Acts 6:1-6-** When the needs were not getting met people were chosen to do the job. They did not let things get overlooked they took care of it.

5. **James 4:17-** Do the good you know. If you do not have all the answers like no one does, then just do the best you know. The more you do that the more you will learn.

6. **Luke 10:30-36-** We all know the story of the Good Samaritan. Why did Jesus say he was a good neighbor? He did something. He didn't do everything he just did something.

7. **Matthew 5:14-5, Mark 4: 21- 22, Luke 8: 16, 11: 33** Don't keep your lamp under a bowl. God wants it to shine. People need to know that you are God's child.

Pray: Ask God for an opportunity to do something great with your life like share your faith.

And tell someone you trust
B-REAL

There was a Shepherd Boy who tended his sheep at the foot of a mountain near a dark forest. It was lonely for him, so he devised a plan to get a little company. He rushed down towards the village calling out "Wolf, Wolf," and the villagers came out to meet him. This pleased the boy so much that a few days after he tried the same trick, and again the villagers came to his help. Shortly after this a wolf actually did come out from the forest. The boy cried out "Wolf, Wolf," still louder than before. But this time the villagers, who had been fooled twice before, thought the boy was again lying, and nobody came to his aid. So the wolf made a good meal off the boy's flock.

tomsdomain

You need to B Real. Just talk about it.
You need to talk when:

You feel beat-down and   Burdened
When you need to be   Reassured
When you feel   Embarrassed
When you experience something   Amazing
When you are thrown a curve ball by Life

Have you ever been so stressed out at work that you just had to talk about it with someone else? Have you ever had to do something important but you just needed a second opinion? Have you ever messed up something you know shouldn't have? Did you ever see a really good movie that you just kept talking about? Have ever just felt like, "What is going on, God?" These are all normal feelings that everyone goes through. And it is normal to talk about them. We don't have to put up a front.

Jesus said I tell you the truth about 30 times in the book of Matthew alone. Since Satan if the father of lies we need to stay as far away from his language as we can. So obviously, the opposite of lies is the truth.

I used to love to lie when I was in high school. I would go out with friends and just make up stories about anything. I would tell girls I was in TV shows like 90210. I would tell people how I was connected to the Mafia so no one would mess with me. I would make up all kinds of excuses for things I didn't want to do. I didn't like the truth very much. But it didn't help my life be very fulfilling.

The famous saying "the truth hurts" has some truth to it. Many people would probably like to hear a lie rather than the truth. *Do I look fat in this? Do you like my new haircut?* Do women really want an honest answer to those questions? *Yes, you look extremely overweight in that outfit. What do you expect, you are actually 25 pounds too heavy for your height, so you probably won't look good in anything you are trying to wear* .Or. *Your haircut looks really bad. You look like a schoolboy that got a haircut from a blind barber.* Men, I don't know if that would go over to well with your wives.

When we tell the truth we don't have to be harsh. In everything we do we have to speak the truth in love. (Eph 4:15) This could be a whole lesson on how to talk to people but it's not exactly that. This step is about talking to people because talking to people draws us closer to God.

Philemon 6 says be active in sharing your faith so you will have a full understanding. As we speak the truth more we understand it more. This applies to many things. When we confess our sins we see how much we need God. When we are open and honest we build deeper relationships. Also, when you tell someone about your faith you understand it more for your self. So just as a normal practice, speak the truth.

We need to be honest with our selves first. The Bible says be careful when you think you are standing firm. (1 Corinthians 10:12) Some people are so deceived, it is scary. It's like the disease of anorexia. Some people who are so skinny already want to lose more weight. People can actually die by believing a lie. Look at 2 Thessalonians 2: 9-11, it is very alarming. So check yourself.

We need to confess and we need to be there to listen to someone confess. Our life is built around relationships, which we will talk about in the next chapters. If we don't build truthful relationships we are actually not living life at all. You are not perfect and everyone knows that you are not, so stop trying to live like you are.

The second main thing I want to focus on in this step is, you need to be real when you share your faith. You need to share your life. I joke around sometimes saying, "You need to share you face." That came from a brother who didn't speak English well. But it is actually somewhat true because you are sharing your self. Your faith is personal it does not come from someone else. So people need to look you in the face and see that you are sincere.

From what I noticed, the doom and gloom stuff usually doesn't help people. Living in New York I have seen and heard a lot of people share about God. I admire some people's boldness (or maybe sometimes insanity), but I can't appreciate their style. If you are screaming in the middle of a subway car, "You are going to Hell!" I don't think many people will want to listen to what you have to say next.

It is probably true that many people on that train are going to Hell, but to me that is not speaking the truth in love. Now Jesus did tell some people they were "Sons of Hell" (Matthew 23:15) but He also saw crowds as "helpless and harassed" (Matt 9:36). I definitely believe there is a time and a place to tell people that if they don't repent they will perish. Jesus tells us a parable about that in Luke 13. Even in that situation, however, He shows His mercy.

I believe now-a-days people want to see a satisfied customer. Everyone has heard about Jesus by now, but the catch is have they heard the truth? The only way people can tell Jesus is true is by your life. If Jesus has fixed you up people will want to see how He did it. Sometimes even with the proof people do not want to believe.

But what I do know is that Jesus does not want us to be like the Pharisees. Jesus was so tough on the Pharisees because they burdened people with rules. Now there are rules and we do need to be obedient to them. But the Pharisees made themselves seem like they were perfect. Nobody likes self-righteousness.

Jesus was the only one who was perfect and He was still the perfect example of humility. So like everything we do and what this whole book is about, let's do what Jesus did. Not the Pharisees, but Jesus. What was His attitude toward the lost? Jesus talks about Himself. He said, "I am the Good Shepard, I am the way, I am the light of the world, I am the Gate." So we need to talk about ourselves and how we follow Jesus.

The truth is we are nothing without Jesus. Talking about yourself doesn't mean that you are trying to make your own disciples. It doesn't mean you want to get people to come to your church. It doesn't mean that your interpretation of the Bible is the right one. It means you share you faith and your faith should be based on Jesus your Lord and Savior.

God set up this world all around relationships. We need to talk with each other to really be fulfilled. (The next 6 chapters will be about different one another relations.) You can use your relationships with others to strengthen your relationship with God.

When was the last time you confessed your sin?

When was the last time you helped someone with their sin?

Are you afraid to do either one?

1. James 5:16- Confess your sins to one another. We tell each other our sin so we can pray for each other not so we can condemn each other.

2. Psalm 51- Be open with God. There are many good Psalms where we can see the psalmist's heart to get open with God.

3. 2 Corinthians 12: 10- When I am weak I am strong. When we put our trust in God and see that He is the only one who can really make a change, that's when change happens.

4. 1 Corinthians 9: 22- To the weak I became weak to help someone be save. We can not come across super spiritual it does not help people and it is not true.

5. Acts 20: 35- You help the weak. It is more blessed to give than to receive.

6. Romans 15:1- Bear with the failings of the weak. We are all weak in some area and we need some one to bear with us.

7. Like 10:2- There is a plentiful harvest of things that need to get done and people who need help. We need to pray for the workers to do this job.

Pray: That your life will be able to help someone to draw closer to God.

Appreciate

Spiritual family

Who is part of your spiritual family tree?

Not physical family, your Family in Christ
These are the people who help you with your relationship with God, your spiritual parents, uncles, brothers, sisters, or children. If this does not make sense you probably need to work on your spiritual family.

Relationships are a huge topic because the Bible tells us in 1 John 2:9 that if we do not love one another we will not make it to Heaven. So relationships are vital to our relationship with God. The majority of 1 John talks about that. So we need to learn how to set up this environment of love in our churches.

Most people I meet don't go to church because of church. The church is supposed to be the place that helps us draw closer to God. But some of us have truly been hurt by someone in church and that has really messed up our view of Christ and those things are really unfortunate. I will address this more in the next chapter. For now let's talk about the regular everyday situations around you.

I am critical by nature. My parents are critical. Their parents were critical and it probably went on for a long list before that. I actually think most of us are critical in some way. Most of us if not everyone is also a little racist in some way.

Read each of these scenarios: You see a young black kid with baggy shorts and an extra large basketball jersey. You see two Puerto Rican guys with gold chains standing in front of a bodega. You see a white guy walking down Wall Street. You see a Chinese guy riding a bicycle. You see a Mexican man walk into a restaurant. You see an Arabian man standing by a taxi-cab. What are you thinking? I didn't make any comments, and some of you are probably saying I am racist by writing those things down. But we think things, we all have our pre conceived notions. All of those guys could be Christian men on their way to study the Bible with someone.

Now, I am white, my parents are Italian, I like a certain type of music, I enjoy certain types of food, I do certain things for fun, but that should never stop me from enjoying everything else that God has blessed me with. I hang out with different types of people I would never have imagined, I enjoy types of music I hated, I eat food that made me sick to look at, I have done so many different things, because I learned to appreciate the people God put in my life.

I still struggle, I'll never say I don't have a racist bone in my body, I still get annoyed by certain people, but that's why I continue to read my Bible and do what God asks me and I can see how He wants to bless me.

Relationships are not easy. As iron sharpens iron one man sharpens another. (Pr 27:17) To help each other out sparks will fly. A brother is born for adversity. (Pr 17:17) People will have conflict; it is normal. If we don't read our Bible it is very easy to get discouraged or give up. You may want to leave church or find another church. But the church is made up of relationships and people are not perfect. You are not perfect. You have plenty of flaws that people could point out about you.

We have to appreciate what we have. We have to fight for our relationships, we can't give up. We have to work out our problems. Again, conflict is normal. If you have conflict with someone it doesn't mean that you can't be friends with them anymore. Appreciate the differences we have. Life would not be fun if the world was made up of billions of YOU. Appreciate your family in Christ because they are a gift from God.

I did a sermon recently for the campus ministry on relationships and the main scripture I used was Ephesians 4-6. Those chapters are full of relationship stuff. I want to start off in Eph. 4:19 speaking the truth in love, we will all grow up in Christ. The goal of relationships is to grow up in Christ. How do you do that? By speaking the truth in love. What is truth? How do we speak it in love?

Here's my little acronym T-talk, R-receive, U-understand, T-teach, H-help.

As we talk to one another we first need to consider others better than our selves and always think the best of others. Many conversations don't go well because we don't assume the best of others. We have preconceived notions of what people are really thinking or of how they are going to say it.

Eph. 4:25-27 says to speak truthfully to one another. We don't need to put up a front. God knows already so we don't need to fake the funk. We are hurt sometimes. It is normal. We just need to talk about it. The Bible tells us not to let the sun go down while we are still angry because that gives the Devil a foothold. We definitely don't need that.

That's also why need to know how to receive. When someone tells us we hurt them what is your first reaction? Verse 29 tells us not to let unwholesome talk come out of your mouth. We just need to build each other up. I made that mistake recently. Someone told me they were hurt by what I did and I apologized quickly and then went right on to rebuking them about why they were wrong for feeling hurt. It was not until I got help that I realized that I probably set up a real unsafe environment for this guy. I had to ask for forgiveness v. 32. Hopefully, he will feel safe to share again.

We have to be understanding too, which is the most important part. Eph. 5:1 says be imitators of God. Wow! God is so much more kind, compassionate, and understanding then we could ever imagine. But we need to understand that. Starting verse 3 up to verse 7 it talks about different sinful behaviors that we can all relate to. We have all been hurt in a different way by sin so we all need to be mindful of that when we interact with one another. Remember where you came from.

The last two things on the list of truth are to teach and help. Verse 8 reminds us that we once lived in darkness. We did not know how to speak when we were in the darkness. Some of us were timid, some were blunt, some were flirtatious, some were rude, some were deceitful, but everyone needs to be taught how to have spiritual conversation. It doesn't come naturally so be humble and get the help.

And that's what relationships are all about, Help. Verse 15 says be careful how you live. Verse 16 says make the most of every opportunity. Use your time with others to help them. You have to be careful; you have to pray for wisdom. Our goal is to edify one another. A great book on this subject is "Closer than a brother" by F. Barton Davis. So let us appreciate one another and get closer than a brother with one another.

Who are your five closest friends?

Why did you choose the people you chose for the family tree?

Are you a good addition to your spiritual family?

1. **Galatians 5:13**-We are free to serve one another in love. We are not free to sin.

2. **Ephesians 5:19 -21-** This scripture starts of by telling us we need to sing to one another because we are thankful and ends with telling us we need to submit. We need to do both of those things in the name of Jesus Christ.

3. **Colossians 3:16-** If the word of Christ dwells in us we can teach and admonish one another with all wisdom, and we can also sing psalms, hymns and spiritual songs with gratitude in your hearts to God.

4. **1 Thessalonians 5:11-** Encourage one another and build each other up. We need to be built up. Some of us are better at that than others.

5. **Hebrews 3:13-** Encourage one another daily, so that no one may be hardened by sin's deceitfulness. Daily means everyday.

6. **Hebrews 10:24-25-** We need to spur one another on to meet together. Sometimes we don't want to meet up but it is beneficial.

7. **1 Peter 3:8-** Finally, all of you, live in harmony with one another; be sympathetic, love as brothers, be compassionate and humble.

Pray: That you will build deeper spiritual relationships.

Don't hate

Bitter roots

Where is your mind!

This is big. Like I said in the last chapter this is a continuation from the last notes. It's actually sort of the same thing; I just needed an extra chapter to get into more detail. When things go wrong in church people blame other people. And this is not only true in church; this is also true everywhere else. Now we can continue to live like this or we can decide to change. Most of the ideas I have or maybe I can say all of the ideas I have in this book are from other people. But I will be the first one to complain about people. Even the people I got ideas from. It is so much easier for me to look at the negative before I can see the positive in someone and most of us can relate to me.

But you don't know who I know. You don't live with my husband. You haven't been hurt the way I've been hurt. You don't understand me, if people would just give me a chance, if people would just listen, if this, if that...

Yeah, I don't know you, I don't know your situation, but I do know you don't want to feel the pain that you are feeling. Some people put on a front like they enjoy the pain. Some people love to hold on to the bitterness. And most of us feel better about ourselves when we belittle someone else. I'm sorry but you have to grow up. This book is about drawing closer to God. If you don't want to do that put the book down now and thanks for reading as much as you did. If you do want to get closer to God, no matter what your situation, you have to get closer to people.

Matthew 18 tells us how to deal with situations. First, you go speak to the person who hurt you. If they don't listen, get someone else. If they still don't listen, get the church. Then after that, you've done your part. The Bible tells us to make every effort to keep the bond of peace. (Eph. 4:3) Too many people I know left church because of people who upset them. Even if it is a good church that they know was teaching God's word correctly. Some will say, *Oh, but this person wasn't there for me in my hard time, I was really counting on them.* Sorry. I know it hurts. I would never put those feelings down, but that's life -- you're going to get hurt. I don't know who told you differently, but it's true.

I was deceived. I thought I would not have one argument with my wife when we got married. Ha! Now do I have a great marriage? YES! Do I get mad at my wife? More than any other person in the world. Do I love my wife? More than any other person in the world. Now I'll get more into marriage in another chapter. But it is the same with other people. If you love someone deeply they will hurt you deeply and vice versa.

One day I heard one person complaining about someone. The next day I heard someone else complaining about the complainer. You are the problem. You have to take responsibility for yourself.

We need to forgive so we can be forgiven. We have to stop being so hard on people. We have to move on. We can't dwell on the past. Life is too short. And let me say it again, you will get hurt. That doesn't mean leave or that the person doesn't love you. It means you are normal. Let go of your past and let God take control of your future.

Summarizing Proverbs 10 it says, "The mouth of the righteous brings life, the wicked mouth brings violence. Hatred brings dissension, love covers over a multitude of sins. Discerning lips are wise. If you lack judgment you will get a beating. Wise men store up knowledge a fool invites ruin. If you hide hatred you have lying lips. Fools slander. A lot of words means sin is near, hold your tongue, a righteous tongue is like silver nourishment" I share this because it takes wisdom to have spiritual conversation. Proverbs 10:31-32, 11:12, 12:16-19, 21:23 all talk about guarding your mouth. It takes a lot of work and a lot of wisdom to guard your mouth. And it is very important to guard your mouth.

Satan can use your words to destroy. If we do not guard our mouth Satan will turn the things we say into weapons of mass destruction. In chapter 3 James gives some great illustrations on taming the tongue. He compares it to taming an animal or a ship. That means that it is going to be hard work. It is not easy to say righteous things all the time.

If you look at people of the world you hear this negativity very clearly. Adults curse at each other over a lost parking space or someone that cuts them off on the road. They gossip and insult people behind their back. The jokes we find funny are usually aimed at insulting a famous person or a specific group. Politicians insult each other to improve their campaign. If our leaders are doing it why shouldn't we?

Children are just the same because that is what they see from the adults. The students I work with in the public schools seem like they don't even have a clue how to compliment someone. They are constantly calling someone gay, stupid, fat, ugly, special-ed. It is very sad. Their favorite form of entertainment is "YO Mamma" jokes. Their second favorite is watching someone get hurt. Those are the two most enjoyable things for my students and to train this out of them is extremely difficult.

The same goes for us as Christians. It is very easy for us to complain. We complain about the world. We complain about other Christians. We complain about others who complain too much. It takes training. We have to practice saying positive, righteous things because anything else is from the Devil.

James gives another example in chapter 3 of how fresh water and salt water can not flow from the same well or how one tree cannot bear another type of fruits. So we as Christians have to be an example of how to keep a tight rein on our tongue. There was a famous saying during World War II. "Loose lips sink ships." That is still true today. Loose lips ruin relationships. They give a bad name to Christianity. They cause all types of dissensions and factions. They cause people to hate. If we are Christians that stuff can't come out of your mouth.

Things will happen, people will say something hurtful. Someone will insult you. How will you react? We never want to have a bitter root grow in our heart. A kingdom divided will never prevail. So resolve matters quickly and don't go to bed angry because the person you are hurting most is yourself. God is not happy when you are hurting. He loves you and He wants us to reciprocate the feelings to others.

What bitter roots do you have?

What makes it hard to live in peace with every one?

Who do you have to forgive?

1. **Ephesians 4:31**- Get rid of all bitterness, rage and anger, brawling and slander, along with every form of malice. We all have this nastiness in us so we have to clean it out.

2. **Ephesians 4:2**- Be completely humble and gentle; be patient, bearing with one another in love. It takes humility to bear with others mistakes

3. **Ephesians 4:32**- Be kind and compassionate to one another, forgiving each other, just as in Christ God forgave you. It also takes humility to forgive.

4. **Hebrews 12:15**- See to it that no one misses the grace of God and that no bitter root grows up to cause trouble and defile many. When we allow the bitter root to grow we will miss God's grace

5. **Colossians 3:13**- Bear with each other and forgive whatever grievances you may have against one another. Forgive as the Lord forgave you. We can forgive because we were forgiven.

6. **James 4:11**- Brothers, do not slander one another. There is no benefit to slander anyone; it only makes you more critical.

7. **Titus 3:3**- At one time we too were foolish, disobedient, deceived and enslaved by all kinds of passions and pleasures. We lived in malice and envy, being hated and hating one another. But we don't live that way any more.

Pray: That you will get rid of any bitterness in your heart towards anyone.

Date

Building in the Kingdom

James' top ten list of cheap dates in New York

10. $20 find a restaurant that has a special deal and have a great time of fellowship (prepare some questions in advance, save money for a tip)

9. $15 nice dinner in the house – rice, fish and juice; play a fun game

8. $10 pasta night - pasta sauce, soda and draw or paint

7. $8 picnic in the park – sandwich, a bag of chips and a case of water, you will use two bottles for each of the next dates and you can even share some with your double

6. $7 flowers - go to botanical gardens, it's free at a certain time

5. $5 hamburgers and fries from the dollar menu at McDonalds

4. $4 get two hot dogs downtown and go to the American Museum of Natural History (they only ask for a suggested donation)

3. $3 get two slices of pizza and see a free concert in the park

2. $2 buy two bars of ice cream from the bodega

1. PRICELESS - tell the sister you will fast together for a great cause and pray in Van Courtland Park

In talking about relationships I have to talk about dating. Most people I have spoken to about this subject have been hurt really bad by a person of the opposite sex. So this usually causes them not to trust the opposite sex. Most or should I say all of these bad situations usually occur when people are not applying biblical standards to their relationships.

Now dating is not spelled out specifically in the Bible but there are plenty of principles that we can apply. The first and most important is 1 Timothy 5: 1-2 "Treat young men as brothers and treat young women as sisters with absolute purity." Absolute purity is a high calling but with God everything is.

We live in a society where absolute purity is not even close to what their standard is. I would say absolute lewdness is the standard. Women are portrayed as sex symbols. Songs and music videos totally degrade women. The clothing that is popular now is low cut, too tight, and too short. And men are considered "Playas" or "Mac Daddies" if they sleep around. Young men walk around with their pants low flaunting their underwear. And it would be very rare to be in a conversations with high schoolers were there is no profanity.

I could go on and on how the purity of the world has been quickly declining. It wasn't very long ago when certain things were not allowed on TV and now they are considered perfectly acceptable. But they can not be acceptable to us as Christians. Young men and women have to take a stand against the world if they consider themselves to be Christians.

Many marriages and families are falling apart because Satan has set up a delusion and many people are falling into his trap. I went to the NY botanical gardens today and I saw an older woman wearing a shirt saying "I'm bringing sexy Back". I want to change the words of that shirt to say I'm bringing purity back. That's how God set it up and that is how we need to keep it. Purity is normal.

Now we can still change our mind if it has been tainted. The world sets up a fantasy that is not reality and we are disappointed when we don't achieve that in a relationship. The romance we see in the movies or read in books is fiction. Grow up and stop seeking after that. Prince Charming is not going to sweep you off your feet on his white horse. And fellas, if someone introduced you to pornography at a young age your mind is totally warped.

I hate that many of us had to experience all of this negative stuff but I think some of us would not have understood God's love if we were not hurt by someone else. I know I needed to get hurt to appreciate God. But now that we have established that the world's view of relationships is off, what does a normal relationship look like? Dating can be a very tricky subject. Opinions can change from person to person. So I will give you some scriptures that relate and some situations that I have learned from, and I feel are best practices.

Now like everything else in this book I am talking about Christian dating, so we are not talking about "macking the honeys" or "scoring". We are talking about pure spiritual dating. First off I think dating is good, I think it is normal, and I think it is fun. As a single Christian I went on many dates, most of them were with sisters that I had no interest in marrying. I have a bunch of memories of dating as a Christian, some better than others but none that I regret.

First of all I think Christians should date Christians. Believers should not be yoked with unbelievers. (2 Corinthians 6:14) Dating is a close relationship, so I believe we shouldn't date someone who has a different standard. You want to have spiritual dates. As Christians everything we do should be spiritual. That doesn't mean that all you do is talk about how great God is and how much you love church. (Even though that would probably be a great date.) But at least pray for your food, share what you are learning in your Bible, and practice spiritual qualities (patience, kindness, self-control...)

To me it does not make any sense not to date a Christian. Proverbs 6:24-32 tells us to watch out for the prostitute. I'm not saying that everyone that is not a Christian is a prostitute, but I am saying it can be just as dangerous as going out with a prostitute. There is so much more temptation. If Jesus is not Lord then what is? Is it your emotions? If it is then I surely don't trust it. We are wild animals at heart. If we are in the heat of the moment and there is nothing or no one to regulate us we can let our emotions get the best of us. So be very, very careful.

Another old school tradition I believe in is double dates. Number one it protects and number two it is more fun. I also encourage brothers never to be alone in a closed space with a sister who is not your wife. There is no need to give Satan a foothold. I don't care how strong you think you are. Samson was the strongest man and he got punked by little Delilah.

The more the merrier. When you are single you really don't need to get that deep with a person of the opposite sex. It is those emotions I am talking about again. Once you start getting deep your mind starts to play tricks on you. I remember once as a young Christian I was driving a sister home from a group date and I got lost. Conversation was going well for a while but as we stayed in the car for longer trying to figure out where to go and as it grew later and I grew more tired, the conversation grew deeper. By the time I had finally dropped the sister off I had thought we made a soul connection. My mind played tricks on me for a long time. I had to fight to recreate a normal relationship with this sister. Thank God it did not get serious.

Dating the right way works and it is fun. Things don't need to get weird. We make things weird. We think we know what we are doing and we mess things up. Set up some simple boundaries for yourself and enjoy all the benefits of this world that God has blessed you with.

If you are married this still applies to you. Have fun set up time with your spouse. You can even invite some singles over your house for dinner. Dating shouldn't stop. It should be a relaxing break from the everyday routine. So let's have a great time on our next date.

How is your purity?

How can you purify your mind from fantasies?

What are you looking for in a mate?

1. **Deuteronomy 22:13-20-** Sexual sin ruins a relationship, that's why rules were so harsh and specific in the Old Testament.

2. **1 Timothy 4:12-** Don't let anyone look down on you because you are young but set an example for the believers in speech, in life, in love, in faith and in purity. Your purity should be an example at any age.

3. **1 Timothy 5:2-** Treat older women as mothers, and younger women as sisters, with absolute purity. Understand the relationships.

4. **1 Peter 3:2-4-** The purity of your life will help others to get to know God. Stay Pure for God's sake.

5. **2 Corinthians 6:14-** Do not be yoked together with unbelievers. We cannot have to close relationships with those who are not Christians.

6. **James 4:4-** Friendship with the world is hatred toward God. Anyone who chooses to be a friend of the world becomes an enemy of God. You need to be spiritual

7. **Proverbs 5-** This Proverb is a huge warning against adultery. Messing with the opposite sex in noting but trouble.

Pray: That you will go on a fun date soon and encourage someone.

Step 17

Wait

Courting

TESTING YOUR PATIENCE?

Traffic

On line in a
bank

Waiting for a bathroom
stall

At the doctor's office

YOUR PERFECT
SOUL MATE

The last chapter was on dating. This chapter will deal with courting. Dating is fun, no strings attached. As you are dating you should start to see who you enjoy spending time with. Then you will go on another date and maybe a few more. Once it gets to that point and you would like to date one specific sister every weekend, I call that courting.

Now courting shouldn't be a rash decision. It should be done with a lot of prayer and advice. In my opinion this step should lead to marriage. And marriage is the second biggest decision you will make in your life right after becoming a Christian. So if courting is the start of it, you better take your time to make the best choice. Again some people will disagree with me, as they think that having a girlfriend in no big deal. I am not here to argue just to let you know some spiritual hints.

Any decision as a Christian should be well thought out. We also have the Holy Spirit that should guide our steps. So especially with a decision on having a girlfriend, it shouldn't be a *whatever* thing. I know we live in America and certain things are no big deal to us, but in terms of our track record with dating and marriage, we are not even close to a good example of what relationships should look like. I was born and raised in New York and I had my share of mess-ups in dating the short time I did before I became a Christian. So I was not at all thinking that I had it figured out when I came into God's kingdom. I think a big problem is that most of us think that we've got it figured out and that's where the trouble begins. God opposes the proud but gives grace to the humble. (1 Peter 5:5) Get advice about who, when, how, why, and what to do when you go steady. (Proverbs 12:15) God will just bless the humility of you doing so. And don't just ask the people who you know will tell you what you want to hear. Ask to get some deep insight. (Proverbs 19:20)

First of all you need to ask God. Pray deeply about it. The Holy Spirit will lead you if you are listening. Now don't mistake your emotions for the Spirit. It might feel the same at times but they are two totally separate things. Many times, just like it happened in the Bible, God uses spiritual people to tell you what the Spirit is trying to say. We are sometimes blinded by these situations. So it takes someone else to point it out to you. (Proverbs 20:18)

But you don't understand how we feel about each other. We are meant to be, I feel it. This has to work; I don't know what to do without him. Those are all scary words and can lead to big trouble because it does not give the Spirit room to move.

I have seen too many sad situations because people don't listen to advice. A close friend of mine had a beautiful relationship going on. He was given some advice he didn't like. He left and got married in another state to someone else. He says he's happy, but what about the sister you left over here with false hopes. I just found out that another good friend starting going steady, the next thing I know he was engaged, and the next thing I knew they broke up. Wow, those emotions are quick! Others who rushed into marriage don't live together, others who didn't take advice argue constantly and struggle financially, and others who were serving wholeheartedly barely make it to church. These are all friends from church that I know personally. I'm not talking about the world. Choosing the right mate will make you or break you.

Sometimes it can be the right one but not just the right time. Now every situation is different. My courting experience is a book in itself. I am not even going to attempt to get into it. We got a lot of advice and sometimes it didn't all add up. But God usually uses relationships to test your character. Some relationships come easier than others but if you get your mate without a fight I would anticipate some rocky waters in the future. Anything worth something has a price. It wasn't easy for me to become a Christian. It wasn't easy for me to write this book, and it wasn't easy to have the relationship I have with my wife.

I have a lot to say on this topic. Above all else it has to be a spiritual decision. That means study things out. Pray. Get lots of advice. And strive to be righteous. Now some of you are past Steps 16 and 17 but you can still use those experiences to evaluate where you are today. Some of you may have gotten married before you became a Christian. We all have different experiences. So let's learn from the past and let's help others from our mistake or accomplishments.

Besides just the simple fact of courting and finding the right mate this chapter should also help you to focus on the fruit of patience. James 5:7-10 gives us an example to be patient until the Lord's coming. See how the farmer waits for the land to yield its valuable crop and how patient he is for the rains... as an example of patience in the face of suffering, take the prophets who spoke in the name of the Lord.

The Bible gives us a few examples of patience. Look at Jacob. (Gen. 29) He waited seven years. Twice! That is actually a pretty weird story to me. First he worked seven years before he could get married. That shows patience. That's awesome. But then his father in law gives him the wrong girl to marry. How does that happen? And then he agrees to work another seven for the right girl. That's weird, but it is a great example of patience.

There are also some great examples in God's kingdom today. My friends Chimere and Ayanna's wedding was encouraging. They were Christians from a young age and they waited. They were building for a long time. At times I thought they weren't going to make it, but they did and they are happily married today serving God's kingdom. Then there is Nicole Lewis and Bim Towolawi. Nicole has been a faithful Christian for many years. I pretty much resolved in my head, *She is one of those sisters who marriage is not for.* And that might be true for some people but it wasn't for her, and she recently came back from her honeymoon with her spiritual husband going right back into the work of the Lord.

God wants to make us happy and He knows how to make that happen. Learn what that means for you. Read some books on dating or listen to tapes if you are at that point in your life. Some suggestions are "Passion and Purity," "I Kissed Dating Goodbye," and "Dating in the Kingdom." But most of all seek God in His word and through prayer.

What are the benefits of waiting?

What are the cons of being impatient?

Name something that you are glad you waited for, or regret doing too soon.

1. **Ecclesiastes 7:8-** The end of a matter is better than its beginning. Be patient, God will work it out.

2. **Colossians 1:10-12-** Be joyful when you are waiting. You know that you are waiting for something great.

3. **1 Timothy 1:16-** Jesus was patient with us we need to imitate his behavior.

4. **2 Timothy 3:10-** You know all about my teaching, my way of life, my purpose, faith, patience, love, endurance. People should know your life.

5. **2 Timothy 4:2-** Preach the Word; be prepared in season and out of season; correct, rebuke and encourage—with great patience and careful instruction. Your life should always be an example.

6. **Hebrews 6:12-** We do not want you to become lazy, but to imitate those who through faith and patience inherit what has been promised.

7. **2 Peter 3:9-15-** Bear in mind that our Lord's patience means salvation. And your impatience might lead to your loss of salvation.

Pray: For patience. (get ready for testing)

Consummate

Marriage

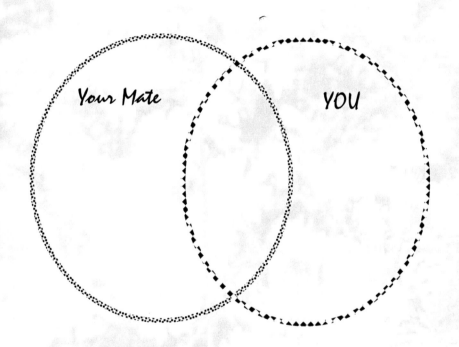

Your Mate

YOU

What are your character traits?
What are your mates traits?
Who are you together?

You can hear a lot of things about marriage. Some are said in fun, some are dead serious, but most things you hear are not good. Now Paul said it was better not to get married and be able to focus on the Lord's work (1 Corinthians 7:28) and in Ecclesiastes the Bible says that two are better than one. Whichever way you look at it, you have to have a spiritual perspective to get the full potential out of marriage.

There are many jokes about marriage and many stereotypes about what men like and what women like. I'm not too crazy about either of those two things. There are many struggles in marriage and there can be major victories or great disasters with marriage so it is really not a joking matter. And I don't agree with most stereotypes; they can be very condescending. I know they are all used in fun, but I will try to stay focused and help you with your closest human relationship.

Marriage is great. It was designed by God in the first book of the Bible, it was part of God's creation story and if you think about it, it makes sense. No marriage, no kids, no future. The story ends after Adam and Eve. But God allows us to continue on. There will be more on that in the next chapter. Also in Genesis 2:24 the Bible tells us to leave and cleave. You leave you family and become one flesh with your mate. It is a deep concept and it builds a powerful relationship.

Let's talk about the stereotypes. All men are not dogs; they can get in contact with emotions, and they do like to talk. Women can control emotions, women do enjoy sex, and women can spend less time in front of a mirror than men. Every case is different and it doesn't make you more man or less woman if feel more one way than another. I had to make that clear before we continued, because you may have already heard some things from other places that have discouraged you. There is no mold for how men should feel or what women should struggle with.

God does give specific roles to men and women. Yes, the Bible says that we are all equal in God's sight but boys have a penis and girls have a vagina. (That's from the movie "Kindergarten Cop") Ephesians 5:22-23 gives us the roles. Men are supposed to lead and love and women need to submit and respect. It's not sexist and it doesn't put down the women. Men don't have babies no matter what you see on Oprah. We have different roles; accept it. The woman can be better at finances and do the bills but the man still leads. The man can be a better cook and be better at cleaning the house but the wife is still called to be submissive.

Now a man leads because he trusts in God and a woman can submit for the same reason. You can not take advantage of this. The marriage will not be successful. The woman who does everything her husband says without speaking up is not respecting him and not fulfilling her role as a wife. God created a suitable helper for Adam. This means that she has plenty of good ideas and plenty of good capabilities to support the marriage. The two have to do their part.

I see too many people who mess this up and do not have successful marriages. Again every marriage is different. Someone might be more creative, someone might be better at math, someone might be more organized, someone might be better at shopping. As a married couple you need to make those decisions together and figure out what will be most pleasing to God.

God wants you to enjoy your marriage. He wants to put you with a mate that will help you make it to heaven. If you are married you can still repent and fix whatever it is you need to fix, and we all have things to work on. Take time out to work on your marriage, it is the second most important relationship after God. Not your friends, not your siblings, not your parents, and not your kids -- your spouse is your number one.

If things are rocky, fix it. Take time out with you and your spouse to become more intimate. You will be setting an example for many people. Marriage is not popular these days. Show the world it can work God's way. You are setting and example for your kids; are you showing them something they want to have.

God often refers to His relationship with us as a marriage. He calls it a great mystery, that the church is Jesus' Wife. (Ephesians 5:32) We are the Bride of Christ. That is cool and it makes sense if we look at the role of a wife; to submit and respect. Jesus keeps His role as a husband by loving and leading.

Song of Songs is a book full of marriage relationships. We can look at it to see how much God loves us or we could also use it as a guide of what marriage looks like. If you are single close your eyes. I did try to read the book as a single but it wasn't that beneficial to me. When you get married there is a whole different outlook on things. When the two become one her body belongs to him and his body belongs to her. There are a few good books that get into more detail about this. ("Friends and Lovers," "Sheet Music," and the "Five Senses of Romantic Love.")

I guess I need to end this chapter talking a little bit about my marriage. I can't get into too much detail as I said earlier because the story is a book itself. At this point of writing this book we have been married for five years. We were both Christians before we got married. We were best friends. We went on a few dates and then we started courting. I didn't use the word courting at the time. I learned it and built my convictions on it as I studied the subject more. We got engaged and then we got married. And I am grateful for every part of it.

I am so grateful for my wife because she is my suitable helper. I would not be the man I am today if it was not for her. It would have been a lot easier to choose another sister to be my wife, because this marriage totally went against our families' traditions. Looking back and looking into the future I am so glad I listened to God who called me to Nnenna.

We do have disagreements. We have hurt each other. We have struggled. But we love each other. We have fun together. We go on vacation together. We eat together. We pray together. We serve together. We learn together. We grow together. We laugh and we cry together. We live for God as one. God has given us marriage relationships to enjoy and help us grow. So be encouraged and enjoy the wife of your youth. (Proverbs 5:18)

What does a good marriage look like?

Why do you think God uses the analogy of marriage so often?

What are some reasons marriages don't work?

1. Hebrews 13:4- Keep the marriage bed pure. Marriage is a sacred thing. Don't mess it up.

2. Mark 12:25- There is no marriage in heaven. So this is a special relationship that can only be enjoyed on earth

3. 1 Corinthians 7: 3-5- Your body belongs to your mate you need to take care of one another.

4. Colossians 3:18-19- Wives, submit to your husbands, as is fitting in the Lord. Husbands, love your wives and do not be harsh with them.

5. 1 Peter 3:1-7- Wives, in the same way be submissive to your husbands. Husbands, in the same way be considerate as you live with your wives.

6. Titus 2:4-5- There needs to be a training for young men and women on how to be a married couple especially now that there are so many bad examples.

7. Revelation 21:2- I saw the Holy City, the new Jerusalem, coming down out of heaven from God, prepared as a bride beautifully dressed for her husband. God compares marriage to Heaven.

Pray: For the marriages of this nation.

Procreate

Kids

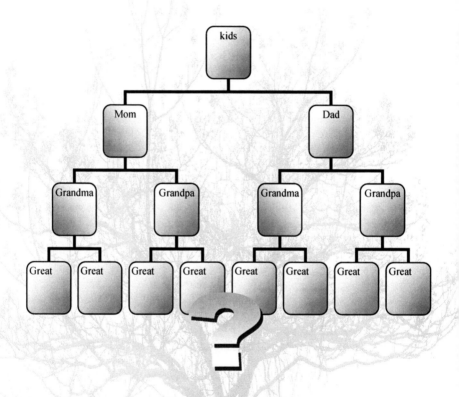

How far back can you trace your family roots?
How does that affect who you are today?

The final step in relationships is children and we saved the best for last. It is actually very funny writing this chapter because I have been working on this book since I was single and every time I go back to revise it I have to change the beginning. First I started of by saying I had no kids, then I said I was going to be a father soon, next I said my daughter was a few months old, and now she just turned 2 and my wife is pregnant with our second child. It feels like yesterday that my daughter was born and I can't believe how much she has changed in a short period of time. And the time is just going faster from here. Children will not always be children forever. So we need to make the most of the time we have with the children we are around. (Proverbs 78:5-6)

Fatherhood has been challenging but it has been incredibly rewarding, and I look forward to watching my children grow up. When my wife and I left the hospital after Victoria's birth, the doctors didn't give us a step by step manual, they didn't give us a test to complete to see if we were fit parents. All they gave us were papers to sign to say we watched a video on not shaking the baby, a few extra diapers, and the bill came in the mail a few days later.

I think one main reason God allows us to have kids is to keep us humble and I believe, more than ever, it is a difficult time to raise children. If it wasn't hard enough already, we now have thousands of conflicting pieces of advice on the Internet that should help but actually makes child rearing more difficult. We have so many programs and TV shows to distract us from quality time with our kids, we have so many bills that most mothers can't afford to stay home. The school systems are getting worse and worse, (especially where I live). Its challenging enough just understanding Victoria, and striving to meet her needs.

There is no perfect book to help you with raising your child because the author of the book never met your child before writing it. The only perfect book we have is the Bible, and it gives us the perfect amount of information we need to know on how to raise our kids. I don't discredit any parenting philosophies but knowledge puffs up and love builds up. (1 Corinthians 8:1) Please don't try to buy into a new idea of *this is the best way to raise you child.* Our parents messed up with us, and their parents did with them, and we still were able to become Christians. I do suggest reading Christian books on parenting that will point you back to the scriptures and give you ideas on how to put them into practice, like *The Quiver, Shepherding a Child's Heat, and The Tender Years.*

Now I don't say this to leave us hopeless. If your children are older and you feel like you have messed up with them God can still fix it. If they are still young, you still have the chance train them in the way they should go and they will never depart from it. (Proverbs 22:6) Most of us had to learn the hard way but our children don't need to.

I teach middle school in the Bronx and most of the time after speaking to a parent I can see why a student acts the way that they do. It is hard for me to expect a student to stop cursing when the parent feels free storming into the school cursing in front of all of the other students. It is hard to motivate students when a parent is comfortable sitting at home collecting a welfare check and not looking for a job when they are perfectly able. It is also sad to see young girls having babies because their parents had them when they are so young. Now that doesn't mean that a single parent can't raise a Christian child. Many single parents I know have a positive influence on their children because they have repented of their sinful lifestyle and are now showing their children what it means to be righteous.

Children are like sponges, they take everything in and it is easy for them to imitate. They usually do what you do and not what you say. It is very hard to tell a child not to smoke and smoking is bad when you are a smoker. It is hard to tell a child not to lie when you tell lies. Our righteous lives are the best things we can show to our children. They don't need new sneakers, the new game system, or to go to Disneyland, all they need is for you to be a righteous example. (Psalm 37:24-26)

We need to love our children. Children are not a burden. Please never make them feel that way. Life has changed big time since Victoria joined our lives. We can't just get up and go as we please anymore, but it's not a burden; it's different. Life changes, we grow, we have different responsibilities. Children are that, a great responsibility. God has given you the honor to mold someone's life. WOW! I hope you are honored not burdened. The disciple didn't get, it do you? (Luke 18:15-16)

Life is not about us anyway. It is better to give than to receive. (Acts 20:35) When we can focus on giving to our children it makes us more grateful. That means all the children we come into contact with, cousins, nieces, nephews, or students. If you don't have any children of your own you should invest in another child's life. Be a positive role model. Train these kids. (Titus 2:6-7)

I love being a father. It gives me a better glimpse of how God sees us as His children, and how He loves us unconditionally. It also helps me to see how much it must have hurt to see His son, Jesus, get killed. Victoria is so dear to me I don't know if I could stand to see her die. The thought alone disturbs me. But Jesus did die. And He died a horrible death, when He didn't have to. And He died for you. That's the next chapter.

But as we wrap up this chapter I want to encourage you to be grateful for the children in your life. Pray for them and pray for the wisdom to mold them the way Jesus would. I want you to understand that you can never take moments back. So make the most of your time. The decisions you make around a child can change their life for eternity. The words that come out of your mouth could change the rest of there life.

Time goes fast. It doesn't stop. You may not have children of your own but there are plenty around looking for attention. You may have an infant but that won't be for long. You may have teen or pre-teens and they will be adults soon. Or maybe you have grown kids and you will be a grandparent. Wherever you are in life you have a responsibility to the children of God. Please take that responsibility seriously.

What do young people see in you?

How often do you pray for the future?

How are you involved with the youth at your church?

1. **Deuteronomy 4:9-** Deuteronomy tells us to teach God rules to our children and our grandchildren.

2. **Deuteronomy 6:7-** Impress them on our children. Our whole lives should reflect God's teaching so the will learn by our example.

3. **Deuteronomy 11: 19-** There is an emphasis on passing on God's law from generation to generation.

4. **Mark 10:13-16-** Jesus said let the children come to me because the kingdom belongs to those with a child like heart. We forget some basic things when we grow up we need to be reminded.

5. **Ephesians 6:1-4-** You need to expect obedience from your children, not because you are the master but because the Bible says so.

6. **Colossians 3:20-21-** Fathers have a unique role with their children that is irreplaceable. They must not take advantage of that.

7. **1 Timothy 3:4, 3:12, 5:10-** Your children have a lot to do with your standing in the Church.

Pray: For the children of our nation.

Focus

THE SON

We are halfway through the book. Some of you might be on track. Some of you might be all over the place. It is so hard for me to be focused so I am sure that a few of you are not focused. I have to believe I have adult ADD. So that's why I include this chapter in the book.

I am so glad I messed up on writing this chapter. What am I talking about? Well, I had set up a plan that I needed to stick to, but I didn't. I just had some quick prayers and mini Scripture readings the last two days. I was pretty much running on my own fuel. And if you are expecting me to say my day was horrible, you're wrong. There are many people who don't focus on Jesus and don't claim to be Christians. Those people sometimes get a lot more accomplished than people who claim to be Disciples of Christ. And that's the scary part.

It is very easy not to focus on Jesus. So many people do it. It is so easy to be consumed with our selfish desires and not think about what Jesus wants. It is so easy to get distracted. You can get a phone call, see something on the Internet that will keep you searching for hours, a video game, a puzzle, anything you can think of can get you distracted. So we need to focus on Jesus daily to stay on track.

Jesus said if you hold to my teachings the truth will set you free. (John 8:31-32) Many people who seem successful are probably not very truthful. I had a hard time being truthful these past two days. Now I am confessing my sin here not condoning it. I was deceitful and disobedient and it actually helped me to get ahead. Just as God gives good gifts, Satan appears to do the same just as he did with Eve in the Garden. If we are not focused on Jesus we will not see that our eternal rewards are more important than getting ahead in this life. Those movies where people sell their souls to the Devil are probably not too far fetched.

Some people might say it is impossible to live without Jesus. Yes, that is true eternally but more people live in this world without Jesus because they are lied to by Satan. Why do I keep on repeating that? Because it's hard work to focus on Jesus and it is a daily decision.

I still believe it is best to start your day, end your day and fill your day with Jesus. Is it legalistic, is it monotonous, is it religious? It may seem like it is those things but if it gets you closer to God, just do it. Of course it has to come from your heart but some days it won't feel easy. Those are the days you need to just do it. Hopefully that is not the majority of the time. I believe if you are consistent with a good habit you will inevitably enjoy doing it.

I do well spiritually when I get up early in the morning. Tomorrow church starts at 10:00 a.m. so I am planning to get up at 6:00 a.m. to focus on Jesus. I should start writing again at 6:30. I'll let you know how it goes.

Remember, we are the light of the world. When a light is focused it becomes a laser beam. So let's get focused and have our light be effective. I can keep writing and writing or you could keep reading but if we do not remember to focus on Jesus, our light will not have the power it needs. Gather your thoughts that you have scattered and look at Jesus.

To get a good picture of Jesus let's look at what He was focused on in His last days from Matthew's gospel and we can see what we should focus on:

26:12 Jesus knew money didn't matter, His purpose was more important

26:20 He knew His obstacles, He knew what would stand in His way

26:26 He gave His whole body to His purpose, not just a little part of Him

26:28 He gave His blood, not just a pint of blood, He poured it out until death

26:31 He was aware of others' weaknesses and warned them about it.

26:34 He gave specifics, He knew what He wanted and how to delegate it

26:36 He prayed and He prayed and He prayed some more

26:37 He took along companions, He was not too proud to ask for support

26:38 He was real, He admitted His struggles, what was on His mind

26:40 He encouraged others to pray, He knew people needed it

26:46 He was focused

26:50 He was still polite in the midst of insults and attacks

26:51 He was not rash, He held on for the right times

26:52 He was cool, no situation rattled His thoughts or His confidence

26:53 He chose the right way not the easy way

26:54 He obeyed the Scriptures, He didn't live by opinions but by God's Word

26:55 He was above reproach, His righteousness could not be questioned

26:63 He did not talk too much, He knew when to keep His mouth shut

26:64 He spoke the truth in love, He had a lot of integrity

26:67 He was self controlled, He did not snap when people instigated Him

27:11 He was honest so He was secure about all of His answers

27:14 He did not argue because He knew the truth, there was no need to fight

27:26 He endured physical pain, He took it like a man

27:27 He stood alone in a crowd, even when no one would back Him up

27:28 He got humiliated, He stood amongst a crowd who despised Him

27:29 He had major headaches and He pushed on, He did not quit

27:30 He was spit on

27:31 He was mocked, they insulted His family, His faith, and His followers

27:32 He accepted help, He did not refuse a hand when He was in need

27:34 He did not take short cuts, if He was doing it, it was going to do it all the way

27:46 He sacrificed everything, He gave everything for you

27:50 He died

28:18 He was raised with all authority over Heaven and Earth

28:19 He commanded us to go out and make disciples, to baptize, to teach disciples to obey Him, and He will be with us always till the end of time

Jesus was focused and He accomplished His mission. He has set us an example and has now left His mission for you to continue.

Are you ready?

How are you doing?

Are you ready to continue Jesus' mission?

Are you focused?

1. **Hebrews 12:2**- Let us fix our eyes on Jesus, the author and perfecter of our faith, who for the joy set before Him endured the cross, scorning its shame, and sat down at the right hand of the throne of God.

2. **1 Corinthians 1:17- 18**- The cross does not make sense to everyone. It only makes sense to those who are being saved.

3. **Galatians 6:12-14**- We can only boast in Christ and the cross. That is our only connection to God.

4. **Ephesians 2:14-18**- The purpose of the cross was to create something totally new in us.

5. **Philippians 2:8**- Jesus humbled Himself to die on the cross. Let us be grateful for that.

6. **Colossians 1:20**- He made peace through His blood shed on the cross. Through that violent act we have salvation.

7. **Colossians 2:14-15**- Jesus triumphs over the world by the cross.

Pray: Thank God for Jesus.

Get up

Leadership / Servantship

Now we see everything that's wrong with the world and those who lead it.
We just feel like we don't have the means to rise above and beat it.
So we keep on waiting, waiting on the world to change.-John Mayer,

The task of leadership is not to put greatness into people, but to elicit it,
for the greatness is there already. -John Buchan

You do not lead by hitting people over the head — that's assault, not
leadership. - Dwight D. Eisenhower

I am reminded how hollow the label of leadership sometimes is and how
heroic followership can be. - Warren Bennis

Men make history and not the other way around. In periods where there is
no leadership, society stands still. Progress occurs when courageous,
skillful leaders seize the opportunity to change things for the better. -
Harry Truman

A leader is one who influences a specific group of people to move in a God-
given direction. - J. Robert Clinton

All Leadership is influence. - John C. Maxwell

The older I get the less I listen to what people say and the more I look at
what they do. - Andrew Carnegie

The first responsibility of a leader is to define reality. The last is to say
thank you. In between, the leader is a servant. -Max DePree

Quotes from- http://leadershipnow.com/quotes.html

We are so lacking spiritual leadership, in the church and in the world. I think there are many factors that contribute to this lack of spiritual leadership and I hope this one step will help break down the obstacles. There is a leader in every one of us, we just have to let the leader out and we need to do it in the right way. Some people may not lead because they don't know what it means. In this chapter I will give three basic principles to help you to lead.

God has blessed everyone with a talent, some very different than others. But whatever the talent is God wants us to use those talents to help others. I will talk more about this in another chapter. That leads us to the first principle to spiritual leadership, which is, "Use what God gave you". Some of us have the natural ability to lead. We may have already had a high position before we became a Christian but that is not most of us. The rest of us were timid, ordinary unschooled men. What God gives every Christian is the Holy Spirit. That means you are now filled with the Spirit of Power. (2 Timothy 1:7) If God gives you that you have to use it.

In Matthew 25:14-30 Jesus tells the parable of talents. Each of the three men had different talents. All God expected of them was to do the best with what they had. He asks the same of us today.

We also have to understand what leadership is not. It is not lording over people telling them what to do. We cannot use the world as our standard of good leadership. The world tells us, you have to step on toes to get ahead. In God's kingdom you have to clean toes to get ahead.

Principle 2 "Leadership is servantship". Jesus came to serve and He was the greatest leader there ever was. (Luke 22:27) He led by example, so we could follow in His footsteps.

The word servant in Greek is Dulos, which is actually translated into "slave". I am glad I can write this book not as a member of the staff but just as a regular slave. So hopefully you can be encouraged to do more. Let me name a few things I've done to give you some ideas. I lead Bible Talks, at my house or other places, we discuss the Scriptures, eat food, and fellowship. Those things need to be set up or it would not happen. I work with the pre teens and campus ministry in the church. I ask people to teach at mid-week and Sunday. I set up different events. I help plan activities for the yearly camps. I meet up with a couple of guys about once a week to help them with everyday issues.

I have been a Christian for only nine years but that is longer than some other people and even if it is not I can still give advice. I make announcements sometimes, do a communion message, bring the sound system to church, call a meeting to organize details, make up surveys to get information, act in play, direct plays, and study the Bible with people. I also make invitations to hand out, organize prayer time, give people rides home, and a bunch of other stuff in between.

I don't say those things to boast but to give you ideas. You can also take care of the communion supplies, like Chukwuma who makes sure that we have the supplies every Sunday. Or you can set up the communion trays like Pat who is at church before everyone every Sunday, or you can usher and be the smiling face that greets me when I come to service like Ernest and Mac. You can facilitate a hospital ministry like Ron who goes around visiting the sick in the hospitals. You can lead security like Gene who makes sure that wherever we meet we are safe.

There are brothers in my church who work full time jobs and still dedicate time to lead ministries. Cerlenox leads the teen ministry and the singing ministry. Franco has directed countless number of plays and made numerous slideshows for the church. Troy has been holding Chemical Recovery meeting for years at 5:00 p.m. on Sundays. There are many other names that I can mention and many other roles that are filled by men and women who have decided to rise up for God.

I know some people are afraid to rise up to a challenge for many reasons. I know I was and I still am. There are still so many other needs in the church that people are not rising up to take the lead. There are also some people who try to do too much and can't do anything excellently.

Our first role is to lead our family to heaven. If we don't do a good job with that it will be difficult to do anything else. And if you are married to a non Christian or have other responsibilities, I am not telling you that that is a reason not to serve. You still have the same ability to serve. But people are afraid of failure even before they try. Some people just need to be trained and don't know who to go to, to be trained. Some people think they are not smart enough or good looking enough. But the truth is, anyone can be made into a good leader.

My third and last principle of spiritual leadership is "If at first you don't succeed, try again." Discouragement can be a huge killer to leadership. There have been so many things that I have tried and put my hand to that I feel like it was turned to trash. I tried to put together the last Easter play we had. What a disaster! I put so much work into this thing and the whole thing got scrapped. It took a lot to recover from that because I felt like a failure. It was hard for me to see where I went wrong. And I wasn't sure if I ever wanted to get hurt like that again. So many things like that come up all the time. Why bother trying, it won't come out good anyway. A sister just tried to put together a slide show for Father's Day and it didn't work out for the service. She had a great heart but she had so much opposition. I just hope she doesn't give up and she tries again.

It is true leaders who will take the blame. Everyone is mad at Bush because we still have troops dying in Iraq. But there is an enemy out there attacking us. Someone has to make a decision. Someone has to take the lead. The spiritual war is stronger than ever. What role will you play, will you rise up?

We need to see that we are all leaders. Look at the leaders in the Bible. Gideon was a leader but he was also afraid and doubted. (Judges 6:15) Moses questioned God. (Exodus 3:11) Joshua questioned Moses. (Numbers 11:28) Peter denied Jesus. (John 18:25) They all their struggles but these guys along with many others became great leaders and God wants the same from you.

What stops you from Leading?

Do you believe God can use you?

Which area do you think He can use you in?

1. **Luke 6: 39-** Can a blind man lead another blind man? If you want to be a leader you need to have a clear vision.

2. **John 21: 18-** Jesus will lead us. When we were younger some one dressed us but now we will be dressed again.

3. **Romans 12: 6-8-** God gave us all special talents to work with. Use what He gave you and do what you are good at?

4. **Hebrews 13: 17-** Obey your leaders and make there work easy. Good followers make good leaders.

5. **Romans 8:28–39-** We are more than conquerors. I am not sure what comes after being a conqueror, but it sounds good. God wants to work to bless you. Have confidence in that.

6. **1 Peter 1:13–16-** It is a high calling to be holy. We need to be obedient children and set our hope on Jesus.

7. **1 Peter 2: 9-10-** You are a chosen people. God chose you to be His shining light. He calls you to be a Royal Priest.

Pray: Ask God to help you to lead.

Get down

Humility / Serenity

You cannot be a leader, and ask other people to follow you, unless you know how to follow, too. - Sam Rayburn

A leader is best when people barely know he exists, not so good when people obey and acclaim him, worst when they despise him. But of a good leader, who talks little, when his work is done, his aim fulfilled, they will say, "We did this ourselves." - Lao-Tse

Humility is the only true wisdom by which we prepare our minds for all the possible changes of life. - George Arliss

Pride is concerned with *who* is right. Humility is concerned with *what* is right. - Ezra Taft Benson

Humility is royalty without a crown. - Spencer W. Kimball (*Improvement Era*, August 1963, Page 704)

[Humility is:] Greatness in plain clothes - Spencer W. Kimball (*Improvement Era*, August 1963, Page 704)

We come nearest to the great when we are great in humility. - Rabindranath Tagore

Humility leads to strength and not to weakness. It is the highest form of self-respect to admit mistakes and to make amends for them. - John J. McCloy

Humility can be a tricky subject but it is an essential character trait to have if you want to be a disciple of Christ. Moses who is basically the father of our faith from the Old Testament was considered a very humble man. (Numbers 12:3) And Jesus who is in the New Testament calls Himself Humble. (Matthew 11:29) You have to be pretty humble to call yourself humble and for it to be true. I say humility is tricky because most people don't get it. Or if they do understand it, it is really hard to put into practice. (Col 2:18, 2:23) The Bible warns against false humility.

Antoine Lee just did a midweek class and he asked the men in the church what the difference was between humility and being a doormat. Most people gave great responses, but one brother didn't get it. He said, "I think there is no difference. I used to be a doorman and I was pretty humble." But others pointed out some great differences. Humility has convictions; a doormat doesn't. Humility does it for God; a doormat does it for people. Humility does it out of courage; a doormat does it out of fear. Humility gets it done with love; a doormat is selfish.

I think that analogy brought out some great points. God does not want people to walk all over us and we don't have to stay quiet just because we don't want to ruffle any feathers. God wants us to be humble towards Him. Two words that can't be separated from Humility are TRUST and OBEDIENCE. To be humble you have to trust God. And to show your trust in God you have to be obedient to His word. That's what made Jesus and Moses humble. They were obedient to His word because they trusted Him.

A great book that I read about this topic is "A Prideful Soul's Guide to Humility." It is one of the most challenging books I have ever read and one of the most important. The book gives several great examples of what humility is and of what it isn't. I can't even start to go into the details, as it would take up too much space. It is a must have for your bookshelf because we will all struggle with pride at one time.

I have heard many people in church joke about how prideful they are. Since when did that sin become a joke? It wouldn't be funny if I said, *I molested a young boy* or *I robbed and raped an elderly woman.* So we shouldn't joke around with pride which is basically the root of all other sins. Pride is the opposite of humility, if you haven't got that already. So let's talk about it but not joke about it.

Pride hurts and pride kills. Pride doesn't want to get advice. Pride is critical. Pride is selfish. Pride is rude. Pride can be loud or pride can be sneaky. Pride can be a necklace, easy for others to see but hard for you to notice. Pride can show itself in many forms. But I know one thing pride is not: a joke.

Satan was thrown out of Heaven because of his pride so if there were no pride there would be no Hell. So if humility is considering others better than yourself, pride would be considering yourself better than others. Satan thought he could do a better job than God. That didn't go over well with the Master of the Universe and it still doesn't.

We have to fight Satan with our humility. So we have to learn humility. Jesus learned humility by suffering. (Hebrews 5:8) Humility will make us do things we don't want to do. Jesus had to pray for hours because He struggled to be humble. It is not easy to die on a cross but He did it because he knew God wanted it. Jonah struggled to be humble too. He tried to run away from God, he complained and tried to plead his case. But God kept pressing because God knows what He wants. He had to put Jonah in the fish's mouth for three days. (A very strange story if you think about it. I would love to ask Jonah when I get to Heaven.) But anyway, he had to suffer to become humble and obedient, just as Jesus did.

Philippians 2:8 says, "And being found in appearance as a man, He humbled Himself and became obedient to death— even death on a cross!" Jesus came down from heaven, became a man, and allowed people to kill Him. That is humble. He had the greatest job in the world; He was up with God chilling in Heaven. It is funny how people can look at their jobs here on earth or their positions and think that they are above some things. Jesus sets the perfect example of having the highest position and still be willing to allow Himself be humbled for us.

Humility will make you do great things. By the world's standards this doesn't make sense. But by God's standards it is the only way. If you are not humble you will not hear God's voice and He has a purpose and a plan for you. If you don't listen to His plan it will be hard to follow. Now you can try to figure things out on your own, but that is not God lifting you up. That is your own strength. God wants us to come to Him in prayer and allow His Holy Spirit to move in us.

That is the way that humility works. You allow your body to be any empty vessel so that the Holy Spirit can fill you up. When you are moving with the Holy Spirit you are moving with the humility. In John 21:18 Jesus told Peter when you are older someone will dress you. He also said you will be lead where you do not want to go. Those two things are very humbling because you are saying that you need help. This tells me that when we are old enough or mature enough we will be clothed in the Holy Spirit and walk is His shoes.

God gives grace to the humble. (Proverbs 3:34, 1 Peter 5:5) and we all need grace. That's why the Bible also says humble yourself before the Lord. The concepts I am sharing in this book are impossible to achieve without humbling yourself before the Lord. It is even more impossible to read the Bible and put it into practice without humility. We want God's grace and we need God's grace, so we need to be humble.

As we bring the plane down for a landing on humility, it is not a mistake that humility comes right after leadership. And I can't stress that point enough, because we don't get it or sometimes don't believe it. Many times leaders are prideful and they give others bad examples. Pride can sometimes look like power. But God says, humble yourself and you will be exalted. (Mat 23: 12, Luke 14: 11, 18:14). Don't be fooled by false humility. Get down so He can lift you up.

What situations cause you to be most prideful?

Who do you think you are better than?

Point out traits of a prideful person you know,
in what ways are you like that?

1. James 1:9- The brother in humble circumstances ought to take pride in
his high position. It is good to be humble.

2. James 4:6 - God opposes the proud but gives grace to the humble. It is
much better to receive grace from God than to be opposed by Him.

3. 1 Peter 5:5-6- Humble yourselves under God's mighty hand. He will lift
you up in the right time.

4. Daniel 10:12- Set your mind to gain understanding and to humble
yourself before your God and your words will be heard.

5. Zephaniah 3:12- The meek and humble trust in the name of the LORD,
so the will be protected.

6. Matthew 18:4- Whoever humbles himself like this child is the greatest
in the kingdom of heaven.

7. Matthew 23:12- Whoever exalts himself will be humbled, and whoever
humbles himself will be exalted.

Pray: Ask God to Humble You. (wow)

Step 23

Stay home
Loyalty / Commitment

When we are debating an issue, loyalty means giving me your honest opinion, whether you think I'll like it or not. Disagreement, at this state, stimulates me. But once a decision is made, the debate ends. From that point on, loyalty means executing the decision as if it were your own. - General Colin Powell

Put on the *company hat*. (Be willing to accept actions that may have a negative impact upon a particular component but are in the best interests of the company as a whole.) - Reginald H. Jones quoted by Harry Levinson and Stuart Rosenthal

Accept the fact that we have to treat almost anybody as a volunteer... - Peter Drucker

That which you or I think is most unique about ourselves we hide. In ordinary discourse, in the normal state, we share our common self, our superficial self. Yet what is most unique about us is what has the greatest potential for bonding us. When we share our uniqueness, we discover the commonality in greatness that defines everyone on the planet. - Robert E. Quinn

What's gonna work? Teamwork! – Wonder Pets

It is amazing how much you can accomplish when it doesn't matter who gets the credit. - Unknown

There is no "I" in "TEAMWORK". - Unknown

Teamwork: Simply stated, it is less me and more we. - Unknown

TEAM = Together Everyone Achieves More - Unknown

The eye can not say to the ear I don't need you and ...... 1 Corinthians 12:21 You are needed, you are part of a family. This is a spiritual family filled with unspiritual people that are saved by grace. I know when I got mad at my parents when I was younger I would pout and say I wanted to change my name. Even if I did change my name it would not change the fact that I am a Franciamore. I have the nose and all to prove it. The same way we are part of God's family. It's in His blood that we get our family name.

When we are talking about being part of a family we are talking about being part of a church. It may seem easy to change churches, and it is. There are plenty of churches to go to. The Bible says there is one church. So that means that is true. When I got baptized, I got baptized into God's Kingdom, where I am planning to stay. I have lived in the Bronx my whole life and right now God has not made it clear to me that He wants me to move so for now I am staying home.

I am not here to knock anyone's beliefs or ridicule different churches. I am just going to share my convictions from the Bible, again. Jesus prayed for unity right before He died in John 17, so one would have to believe that unity amongst God's people is very important. It seems to me, however, that there is more disunity and divisions among Christians than unity.

I grew up going to Catholic Church. When I was part of that church they claimed to be the one true church. Then when I joined the church I am in now some people claimed that this is the one and only true church. Then I started reaching out to people who were Seventh Day Adventists, Pentecostal, and Jehovah's Witnesses and they all said they were a part of God's only true church!?!

Who's right? Thank God it's not about who's right but it's about what's right. And what God says is very clear, we are the ones that get it twisted. And we are at a time right now when Satan has made things very confusing and complicated when God had made things very simple. I don't want to focus this chapter on different denominations and different religions. But if you are reading this book and you are feeling you are not in a church filled with disciples, then pray. God makes things clear.

Now we already said the church is filled with sinners saved by grace. So there is no perfect church because if you found a perfect church and you joined then you would ruin it because you are not perfect. I believe you can pray for God to make it clear even if He has to clean house where you are.

As a young Christian I prayed fervently for God to make it clear if I was in the right church. I started feeling there were a lot of people in my church for the wrong reasons. The more I prayed, the more He revealed. A little while after that the leadership of my congregation changed drastically, members left, and many people had to recount the cost. I was so grateful that God was able to sweep the house clean.

Is the church perfect now? Not even close. But now I can see my calling more clearly and I can be certain that I am not being led by man but by God. The biggest problem with any "church" is when man's doctrine gets involved; things start to get out of hand. As long as God is in control we can have church.

If you are in a church be part of the church. I had a great time teaching the pre teens yesterday. They are the children part of my family, so someone needs to teach them that they are our next leaders. It's not just teachers that are needed. There are many areas to serve or to be part of in church from security to ushers to preachers to administrators and so on. You just need to find your place to fit in.

It is scary when people don't feel needed in church. I feel that is a big reason why people don't do well spiritually. If you are not functioning as a Christian you will feel useless. I urge you to find a place to fit in quickly, if you have not done so already. You are important. You are part of the body.

I am at home right now watching "America's Got Talent." It's a very funny show. People are interesting. I wonder if some people really believe that have talent and then there are others who have unbelievable talents. I am not encouraging you to stay home and watch reality shows. I am talking about using your talents.

Now you don't need to twirl a baton, or do back flips. You have a God given talent. There is something that you can do well because God wired you that way and God put you in this church so you can use your talent. You have to give all you've got to the church you belong to. You are part of a ministry. Maybe that will give you a better perspective. You are part of a mission team wherever you are. Don't be lone ranger. I'm sure you heard the saying there is no I in team. We are doing this together. We are trying to meet God face to face and we are trying to invite as many other people as we can to do it.

Do people know you by name? Do people know who you are? How is your attendance at church? Are you reliable? Can people count on you? These are some simple questions to ask yourself to show if you are on a team. If the results of your answers are not positive change it immediately. Now this is not a popularity test. I'm not even asking if people like you. I am just asking if you have a role. If not, know your role.

Acts 2:42 is always used as a blueprint for what God's church should look like. It first starts off that we to base our church on the teachings of the apostles. Then you have to be devoted to the fellowship, which includes eating. This also had to be a praying group. There is a high standard for God's kingdom. Don't be fooled by anyone who puts up a sign marked church. The church is not the place, the church is the people.

As you continue on in Acts 2:43, you can see the apostles' miracles. The disciples were filled with awe. The believers met together and shared their stuff. They gave money to those in need. Every day they gathered in different places, temples, homes, and other places. They had glad and humble hearts. They loved being together and because of this people wanted to be a part of it. The kingdom is made up of people like you. You are an important part of the body.

What are your talents?

How can your church use you?

Are you happy in your home church?

1. **Colossians 1:18-** Christ is the head of the body. He is our image of God and He has all authority.

2. **Romans 12:4-5-** There is one body that Christ is part of and you need to be part of the head.

3. **Matthew 6:33, Luke 12: 31-** Seek first the kingdom and everything else will be taken care of. The kingdom is a priority.

4. **1 Corinthians 10:17-** We need to participate in the body of Christ. It is something that we are a part of.

5. **1 Corinthians 12:12-27-** The body is a unit. We all have to take part. No one is exempt.

6. **Ephesians 4:1-6-** One body, one baptism, one faith, one spirit, one hope, ONE.

7. **Hebrews 12:28-** We have a kingdom that cannot be shaken. We need not to worry.

Pray: Ask God to help you find you place in His ministry.

Get away
Retreat/ Regroup

VACATION: Two weeks on the sunny sands - and the rest of the year on the financial rocks. - Sam Ewing

To get away from one's working environment is, in a sense, to get away from one's self; and this is often the chief advantage of travel and change. -Charles Horton Cooley

With me, a change of trouble is as good as a vacation. - David Lloyd George

He who rejects change is the architect of decay. The only human institution which rejects progress is the cemetery. - Harold Wilson

If you don't like something change it; if you can't change it, change the way you think about it. - Mary Engelbreit

When we are no longer able to change a situation, we are challenged to change ourselves. - Victor Frankl

Retreat 1. The act or process of withdrawing, especially from something hazardous, formidable, or unpleasant. 2. A place affording peace, quiet, privacy, or security. 3. a. A period of seclusion, retirement, or solitude. b. A period of group withdrawal for prayer, meditation, or study: - Dictionary by Farlex

Regroup - *intransitive verb* -to reassemble or reorganize, as troops after a battle – Webster's Dictionary

Refresh - To revive with or as if with rest, food, or drink; give new vigor or spirit to. – American Heritage Dictionary

"I will refresh the weary and satisfy the faint." (Jeremiah 31:25) Many of the steps overlap. We already read that God rested at the end of His work, which was the seventh step. This step sends a similar message, but it will focus on how to make those times work through out the year. Too many people are caught up in the rat race of life. We can also get caught up in the rat race of Christianity. That's why we need time to retreat, regroup, and refresh.

There are too many situations that are discouraging. I have spoken to many people who are just trying to get by. They are always to busy for everything. They are in school, they are working full time. They are doing this and they are doing that, but they have no time to do what they want and life becomes a big complaint. You are always behind on everything and everyone stinks. That is not the life God wants us to live.

This step of Getting Away is a time of refreshing. I will talk about three types of getaways in this chapter; weekly getaways, weekend getaways, and week-long getaways. I believe all three are necessary each year if you want to get closer to God. Allow me to explain.

Let's start of with the WEEKLY getaway. The average person works five days a week, 40 hours a week and the average person doesn't really enjoy work. (We will talk about that in a few chapters also) But work is work. It is something that needs to be done. Now your job is not the only thing that needs to get accomplished in your 24 hour day. You have chores, you have to keep your house clean, do laundry, cook dinner, put the kids to bed, do homework. The list goes on and on. Then there are church activities, which might be more fun but they are still commitments. You have Sunday service, midweek services, Bible talk, D- time, D-group, Studies, and all other conversations in between. It is a lot and you could get consumed by the everyday mundane routine of things.

So the WEEKLY getaway is necessary. God doesn't want to go through the motions. He said worship me with all your heart, mind, soul, and strength. (Mark 12) You can't do that if you are burned out. You have to schedule some time for refreshing yourself. Scheduling is a key point that we will also talk about in a few chapters. The weekly getaways can also be daily retreats. They can be a half hour a day, an hour a day, three hours on the weekend, or two hours in the middle of the week. You figure it out. It has to be something you want to do. Not something you have to do. Something you choose to do and that you enjoy doing. This means if you had a horrible, hectic week, you know there is at least one activity you are looking forward to. For example: Go bike riding, work out, draw, watch a movie, play a sport, play a game, go to a mall, write in a journal, knit, bake, whatever floats your boat. You need this every week to keep you mind sane. Just like that Sabbath's day rest allows you to lay down your burdens before Jesus. (Matthew 11:28-29)

The second type of retreat is the WEEKEND retreat. I recommend these about three times a year, or once a month is great. The weekend retreat is cool, you can pretty much do this at anytime you wish and it doesn't have to cost much. Again that's why I love living in New

York. I recently found two bus companies that were having a one-dollar bus deal. That's right, one dollar per person each way so that's $2 for travel maybe $3 with tax. The bus left from Penn Station in New York and went to places like Boston and Washington, D.C., which are a little over three hours away and Philadelphia, which is less than two hours away. Those are three great places to visit. Not only are there so many attractions, there are also some great churches there.

That's one of the biggest things I recommend about going away, visiting the other churches. First off if you know someone you can ask to crash at their place. We have had people from out of town churches visit with us and it is a blast. So I'm sure others wouldn't mind. You get to see other preachers, different singing, and a new fellowship. Hopefully that one weekend will inspire you to do something awesome when you return to your home church. Again there are many things you can do for the weekend that are not that expensive and very fun.

The last retreat is the WEEKLONG getaway. These are the ones you have to save up for but these are the ones that you talk about for years to come. I recommend these once a year. Obviously the most expensive of them all, but hopefully it is the most refreshing. When I started writing this chapter I was on a plane coming back from a Mediterranean cruise with my wife. We flew into Barcelona, and then we went to Sicily, Pompeii, Rome, Pisa, and France. It was a great experience and it helped me to see God and as I am writing again two years later, I am preparing for a trip to Mexico at the end of this week.

I'm not trying to sell you a time share. My point is to go away somewhere different to change things up. I love to travel so this is easy for me. I am saving money to travel different places but if it is not in your budget to book a fancy cruise yet, you could go find a mountain or some other place you have not been or a place you have been that you really like.

I know I need to change my scenery; it helps me to refocus. Every adventure has its different perks. Most of my writing is done during vacation (get away) time. I didn't realize how unspiritual I was getting until the end of this trip. I noticed my self praying a lot more because we had to make sure we made it back to the boat on time every day. We would venture out into a different land every day by bus and train hardly speaking the language. I had to pray we would make it back before the boat left. I had to work on planning and making decisions. I realized how lazy I was getting. My wife got sick the last night of the cruise when we were supposed to be packing up. I already decided that she was going to pack, but when she started to throw up; my lazy selfish heart was convicted. I had a lot of fun on this trip but I also learned a lot. God likes to do that, He likes to teach us lessons.

Whatever it is you decide to do, please, for Jesus' sake take some time to Retreat, Regroup, Refresh, and Refocus. Get away from the everyday routine. Don't become a robot. Enjoy this beautiful place call Planet Earth that Our Father Created for us. Don't be afraid to do something different. Someone else has done it before you. Change is good.

When can you spend some good time with God?

Do you have a place close by that you can take quick retreats?

How would getting away benefit you?

1. **Psalm 23-** We know this is a Psalm of comfort. God tells us he will lead us by quiet waters. It sounds so peaceful.

2. **2 Samuel 16:2-14-** When you come from a long journey or for doing a lot of work you need a time of refreshing.

3. **Judges 19:8 –** We cannot always be rushing to do something. Some times we need to just wait and get rejuvenated. Then you will be ready to go.

4. **Psalm 68:9-** You gave abundant showers, O God; you refreshed your weary inheritance.

5. **Proverbs 11:25-** Be generous to others and refresh others and you will be refreshed.

6. **Romans 15:32-** You can get together with God's people and be refreshed.

7. **2 Corinthians 7:14-** We thank God for all the people who help us to feel refreshed and rejuvenated.

Pray: That God will give you times of refreshing.

Come back

Repentance/ Integrity

It's always too soon to quit! - Norman Vincent Peale

Men acquire a particular quality by constantly acting in a particular way. - Aristotle

A liar needs a good memory. - Quintillian

Integrity without knowledge is weak and useless, and knowledge without integrity is dangerous and dreadful. - Samuel Johnson *Rasselas, ch. 41*

What is left when honor is lost? - Publilius Syrus *First Century BC, Maxim 265*

In looking for people to hire, you look for three qualities: integrity, intelligence, and energy. And if they don't have the first, the other two will kill you. - Warren Buffet *CEO, Berkshire Hathaway*

To be persuasive we must be believable; to be believable we must be credible; credible we must be truthful. - Edward R. Murrow

If everyone were clothed with integrity, if every heart were just, frank, kindly, the other virtues would be well-nigh useless. - Moliere [Jean Baptiste Poquelin] *Tartuffe, V, i (1622-1673)*

To do so no more is the truest repentance. - Martin Luther

Of all the acts of man, repentance is the most divine. - Thomas Carlyle

You cannot repent too soon, because you do not know how soon it may be too late. - Thomas Fuller

Come Back? What is this all about? There seems to be a few different thoughts all meshed into one chapter. So I hope it ends up making sense to you. The first and most basic thought is that you can't stay on vacation forever. You have to come back. The last two thoughts are repentance and integrity. To me they go together because we were all messed up so it takes integrity to repent and to stay repented.

Let's break this down some more. I actually finished reading the book "Repentance" by Ed Anton on my vacation to Europe. So on my way back to New York after reading a repentance book is a great time to think about this chapter.

One of the first definitions I heard for repentance, when I was studying the Bible, is "Repentance is a 180 degree turn." That's one reason why this book is 180 pages, to remind you that at the end of this book God is calling you to repent. 180 degrees means if I am walking one way I turn around and walk the totally opposite way. So all the time we hear repent in the Bible God is calling for a drastic change. "Repent for the kingdom is near". "Repent and be baptized". "Repent or Perish". Strong words with a strong calling.

A lot of times we will need to figure out what we need to repent of on a retreat. That's why I put this right after that chapter, but if that doesn't help the next chapter is about fasting and that is usually a big part of repentance. So the first thing, like the first step of the book is to see what we are repenting of. If we don't know what's broken how can we fix it? Paul is a great example of this. He tells us in 1 Timothy 1:16 that he is the worst of all sinners and he goes on to make a list. Even in Acts 26 where he is struck by the bright light. He says that he has persecuted and killed Christians so now he wants to give back. He saw how much bad he did so he was compelled to repent and go in the totally opposite direction. He who is forgiven much loves much. (Luke 7:47) I think this is very true.

In Mark 10:17-31, the rich young ruler came up to Jesus and he gave Jesus a pretty good resume of what he had done well. He would be someone I consider to be a "Good Guy" but Jesus tells him no one is good but God alone. Then Jesus calls him to repent. Live a totally different life then what you were living. "But I'm good, why should I do a 180 degree turn? Can't I just donate some money or help an old lady across the street?" "Nope, sell everything and repent." It is a tough calling. It is actually easier for a camel to go through the eye of a needle.

The best stories or testimonies if you want to call it, are the ones where people who repented of one way of life and started living for Jesus. I say that anyone can write their own book because everyone's life is a story. We just hope it has a happy ending.

The second part of this step is integrity. Repent and live for Jesus. We already discussed that Jesus always spoke the truth. In fact, He was the Truth. And that's a huge part of integrity. Peter is a great example of this. He is the one who questions Jesus after His interaction with the Rich Man, but Peter had to repent himself, even as a disciple. Some people are so shocked when they blow it as a Christian. You are not invincible to sin when you become a disciple. 1 John says you would be lying if you said that. Obviously the goal is not to sin but when you do repent.

When I study the cross with people I usually look at two people's reaction to Jesus' death; Peter and Judas. They were both Jesus' disciple, they both denied Him before He died, and they both felt bad about it, but they both had two totally different reactions when they messed up. Judas had worldly sorrow and Peter had godly sorrow. Judas killed himself, but Peter wept bitterly and later saved others.

Which story would you like to tell of your life? Again you are not going to be perfect but we aim to be.(1 Corinthians 13:11) As we shared earlier, usually your struggles are what help people to be converted to Christ. Notice I said struggles. Struggles are good, they mean you are fighting and growing. Don't try to inspire someone by saying, *Yeah, I understand, I can't quit smoking either, good thing God is a merciful God.* No, you need to share, since God is so merciful and He spared your life even though you continually sinned, you can stand here today a changed man. Inspire people and show them that they can do it.

I know I messed up and I know I am going to continue to mess up but I want to be able to show people what being a Disciple of Christ looks like. I hate hypocrites, Jesus hated hypocrites and you hate hypocrites, but that is still one of our biggest struggles, being a hypocrite. "Do what I say and not what I do." Or the famous "Sunday Smile" that is nowhere to be found the rest of the week. No matter who's around, God is always watching.

I am glad I have lived in the same area my whole life because it makes it that much harder for me to mess up. Most people that know me know I claim to be a Christian. So I am sure they are looking for things to say, *Hey, I told you this Christianity thing is fake.* I have to watch what I'm doing even when it is easy to lie or to steal. I have to be righteous because that's the story I want to tell with my life. Because even when I am not even close to home I usually bump into someone I know from somewhere. God keeps me on my toes.

Even if you don't know the people you are around, you need to be righteous because that could be the person who wants to know God and your story could be the one that helps that person repent. I want us to understand that the best way for us to help anyone is to show them an example of Jesus. In John 14:12 Jesus tells his disciples that they will do greater things them Him. The only reason this makes senses is that we are able to be in more place than Jesus. There are many Christians who are acting like Jesus so that give people many more opportunities to see Him.

So hopefully you have already repented of major things in your life but I hope you don't think that is the end. Every day is another chapter in the book of your life and any day can be the last chapter. Is it a good story right now? Are you happy with how the story is progressing? If you are not happy, repent. People are watching the reality show of your life. I hope what they see is bringing glory to God.

Do you understand repentance?

Do you understand Grace?

What can people say about you?

1. 1 Kings 9:4- We need to walk with integrity of the heart. I wish some of our fathers were better examples for us.

2. 1 Chronicles 29:17- God looks into our heart and if He sees integrity then He is pleased

3. Nehemiah 7:2- If you have integrity and fear God, He will put you in charge of many things.

4. Job 2:3- God told Satan that Job is blameless and upright, a man who fears God and shuns evil. Could he say that about you?

5. Psalm 25:21- Integrity and uprightness will protect you, if you have hope in God.

6. Psalm 41:12- With integrity you will be in God's presence. You can walk securely with Him.

7. Titus 2:7- In everything set them an example by doing what is good.

Pray: That your life story will be an example to others.

Go fast

Sacrifice/ Self discipline

Sure I am a religious man who is also passionate about conserving the environment. But I am also a CEO, with all the bad habits and attitudes that are natural to the species. . . . I am still naturally self-interested, overconfident, full of pride, and eager to control a meeting as any CEO in America. Every day, I struggle with my ego. - Tom Chappell, *Managing Upside Down*

The first and best victory is to conquer self. - Plato, *Greek Philosopher*

You can never conquer the mountain. You can only conquer yourself. - Jim Whittaker

Talent without discipline is like an octopus on roller skates. There's plenty of movement, but you never know if it's going to be forward, backwards, or sideways. - H. Jackson Brown, Jr., *Author*

It is not enough to have great qualities; We should also have the management of them. - La Rochefoucauld

A man without decision of character can never be said to belong to himself . . . . He belongs to whatever can make captive of him. - John Foster, *Author*

If we don't discipline ourselves, the world will do it for us. - William Feather

I fast for greater physical and mental efficiency. - Plato

Through fasting. . .I have found a perfect health, a new state of existence, a feeling of purity and happiness, something unknown to humans. -Upton Sinclair

Fasting is good for us. It builds character and self-discipline. Now I did not go into an in depth study for this chapter, I am only going to share my experiences with fasting and how it draws me nearer to God. As I hope you already know the purpose of you reading this book is for you to use these steps to draw closer to God.

There are different ways I have fasted, different things I fasted for. When you fast it needs to be for a specific reason and purpose. As I was working on this chapter over the last few years I used the opportunity to fast 3 different times. I will share the experiences and hopefully they will help you.

Today I am fasting for clarity in my life. As I said earlier, one of the reasons I am writing this book is to help me in my walk with God. The main thing I am fasting for is to be able to find a new job. I am not going to eat or drink the whole day, that means, from when I wake up until when I go to sleep I will not eat or drink. (I did take my vitamin this morning.) I also aim to pray or read my Bible to replace the times I feel hungry. Maybe for some people this fast will be too much or maybe it's not enough. Each person has to do what they feel is a sacrifice. God tells us that He desires mercy not sacrifice so we are really not sacrificing so God can be proud of our suffering. (Hosea 6:6)

Fasting is for us and we need to make sure we set up spiritual time throughout our fast. I know there are sometimes I can go several hours without eating just because I am busy, but that is not the purpose. This is a time to focus on God. I have to give up drinking when I fast because I desire drinking the most. So every time I taste my nasty breath I think of the purpose of my fast.

Some fasts end up great and some I get so distracted. This fast went well. I got a job at a school that is a five minute walk from my house. It gave me a spiritual focus but it also gave me an answered prayer.

I am fasting again writing this chapter. I feel compelled every time I talk about fasting. It's good for me. Even though I have a headache and I feel extremely weak, I feel focused; focused on God.

I love to eat and it is so easy to eat in New York since you are never more than five minutes from food, probably even less. Even now with the economy so bad you can still get a snack and a drink for one dollar. So making the choice not to eat builds character. By fasting you are making a choice and saying I have control over my body. If you can keep yourself from eating, I think you can keep yourself from doing other things.

Another benefit to fasting is that you can hear God talk. Fasting never comes alone. You need to fast and pray. Instead of eating you are praying or looking through the Bible. When you do that you can hear God's voice. You get weak so God can be strong. God's Holy Spirit will fill up your body. There are so many other things that can fill up our bodies when we are not thinking. The radio (different advertisements or songs with the wrong message), the TV (different images that cause you to lust or envy), or your co-workers (you hear the gossip and build up bitter roots and evil thoughts). It's better to listen to God.

This is the third day I am fasting writing this chapter. I am pretty much on the home stretch of this book. So my fast now is that I can finish this book and get it published. This was a lot harder than I thought. It took a lot of prayer and fasting. The main thing I think of when I talk about fasting is sacrifice. The definition I like most about sacrifice is giving up something for something else that is worth more.

Yesterday morning while eating breakfast I flipped through the channels of the TV. It took me almost one hour to eat breakfast. What a waste of time. So today as part of my fast I am not going to watch TV. Instead of wasting that hour like I did yesterday, I could use that hour to write. I actually messed up because I wanted to fast TV for 40 days while writing this book. I know I would have gotten a lot more accomplished.

TV is actually something we always need to be mindful of. It can take up our time on a daily basis. I am reading a book called "Moments Together for Couples" by Dennis and Barbra Rainey with my wife. The other day we read the devotional about the number one threat to the family. They said 36% of people at their Family Life conferences said TV was the number one threat. They also shared a statistic that said there are more families with a television in their house than there are with indoor toilets. Wow!

That's a little bit of a side note but the Scripture they shared was convicting, Psalm 101:3, "I will set no worthless thing before my eyes; I hate the work of those who fall away; it shall not fasten its grip on me." We can not let this world fasten a grip on us. The same goes for food. The Bible says food for the stomach and the stomach for food. We should not be mastered by it. (1 Corinthians 6:12-13)

We need to take these times where we give everything to God with no distractions. Come to God stinky breath and all. Here I am, Lord, send me. (Isaiah 6:8) there is something very moving about that. I can't really imagine the scene where Jesus fasted for 40 days in the desert. (Matthew 4:2) After fasting forty days and forty nights, He was hungry. I think hungry is an understatement. Fasting for two days without food and water did a number on my stomach.

I know we are not Jesus but we could fast some thing for 40 days. I once fasted TV, meat, my car, juice, the radio, snacks and maybe some other things I can't remember. I think it is great to develop the self-discipline to say No to something you love for 40 days. I don't know if it is officially a fast if you don't drive your car for 40 days. But it will help you to appreciate your car more. It will also give you an opportunity to reach out to more people on the buses and trains.

Just like Jesus was transformed after His fast I pray that you will be transformed after your fast. In fact, I am going to pray for everyone right now who picks up this book and decides to fast. I pray that you will grow closer to God than you have ever been in your whole life. I pray that you will do the same for others. What a wonderful world this would be if we gave up things that were not necessary for things that really mattered.

When was the last time you fasted?

When will you spend a good time fasting?

What will you fast for?

1. **Acts 13:2-3** – We need to fast and pray for the wisdom to choose the right people for the job.

2. **Acts 14:23**- Any big decisions should be done with prayer and fasting, to ask God for clarity.

3. **Luke 5:33-35**- We will have times of fasting but not all the time.

4. **Luke 18:12**- Fasting is not a time to show off. It is our personal time with God.

5. **Matthew 6:16 -17**- We don't need to look like we are fasting when we are. Don't walk around talking about how hungry you are.

6. **Jonah 3:5**- We can fast as a group. If there is something as a big group we want to fast for we can be unified in the matter.

7. **Zechariah 7:1-5**- Ask your self, was it really for me that you fasted?

Pray: For a miracle.

Slow down

Organized/ Chaos

If you chase two rabbits, both will escape. - Unknown

What people say, what people do, and what they say they do are entirely different things. - Margaret Meade, *Anthropologist*

The indispensable first step to getting the things you want out of life is this: decide what you want. - Ben Stein

Decide upon your major definite purpose in life and then organize all your activities around it. - Brian Tracy

Keep focused on the substantive issues. To make a decision means having to go through one door and closing all others. - Abraham Zaleznik

Patience means living out the belief that God orders everything for the spiritual good of his children. - J I Packer

The two most powerful warriors are patience and time. - Leo Tolstoy

When you make an efficient choice in moments of indecision, you establish more effectiveness within a given time span, saving energy and stress. That's a time shift. - Doc Childre, Freeze-Frame

I have not failed. I've just found 10,000 ways that won't work. - Thomas Alva Edison

The bend in the road is not the end of the road unless you refuse to take the turn. - Anon

Character cannot be developed in ease and quiet. Only through experience of trial and suffering can the soul be strengthened, ambition inspired, and success achieved. – Helen Keller

The last step in the section of the paradoxes of life is Slow Down. After you Go Fast you must Slow Down. Life moves so quickly, especially in New York. As we talked about a few times, you can get caught up in the motions and just zoom through life. We always want to *do*. We always want to *go*. Slow Down. James tells us in chapter 1:19 to be quick to listen and slow to speak and slow to become angry. We become easily angered and discouraged. I think the main reason we become angry is because we want to be perfect. (2 Cor 13:9) It is OK to make mistakes.

"What good is it for a man to gain the whole world, yet forfeit his soul?"- Mark 8:36 Looking at all of this stuff can be overwhelming. When you see the many things you need to work on you might not know where to start. Start somewhere not everywhere. The goal of the book is not to gain the whole world. Your soul is more important. It is a step book, so take one step at a time. You are not racing against people so never compare yourself to other people.

"He has his Master's degree so I need my Master's degree"

"She's married already so I need to be married"

"He already bought a house so I need to buy a house"

That's called keeping up with the Jones'. Even though we don't know who the Jones are, we try to be better than them. We will never be better than them. They don't exist. And the grass is not greener on the other side of the fence. There is no grass, we live in New York, there is just concrete.

But we can't get overwhelmed with all the things we need to do. We need to come up with a plan. This chapter is written because I can get easily overwhelmed. I don't know if you can relate. I think some people might be the opposite and see all of these things that need to get done and do nothing. They are probably motivated by the same thing, being overwhelmed. Some people might be totally lazy, but I don't think that is most people.

If you tell someone do ABC, this is how you do it, this is how long it will take, and this is the reward you will get in the end. I think most people would do it if they like the reward. When people are not sure what to do, or how to do it, or how long it will take, or what the results will be, they get scared. If everyone was like that we would never succeed in life. We need to be strong and courageous like Joshua 1:9.

For the regular everyday stuff we still need to be strong and courageous but we also need to schedule things or things won't get done. Now a schedule is never set in stone. There always needs to be a lot of wiggle room. This might sometimes postpone your plans or it might help you get it done quicker. Like today, I have extra time to work on my book because our daughter went to sleep earlier so we were able to accomplish stuff last night.

Jesus was focused but He still did some side things and sometimes the side things are more beneficial. When we do anything we need to leave some extra time, especially to share our faith. I believe one the biggest reason people don't help others is because they feel to busy. I

116

saw a special on 20/20 or something that proved this point. Also recently in the news a man got hit by a car and it took 20 minutes before someone helped him. Another news story told of a lady who died in a hospital after lying in the waiting room for one hour. So many people passed by but did not help. We can never be to busy to help someone.

I think it is great to plan. As humans we like to get stuff done. When we graduate or finish some project we can rejoice and say we're done. So if we plan things we can do that every day and say that we are done with something. I now have a white board in my room that my wife and I use for planning. I love this idea because when I get something done I could just erase it from the board and I feel a sense of accomplishment.

Planning is not my strength. I have had to pray about this so many times and I am still nowhere close to where I want to be with my organizational skills. I think I can say that I am also nowhere near where I used to be. It takes time to get into a routine that works. What works for one person may not work for someone else and what works at one time may not work at another time. That means we are always evolving.

I am a teacher so that means I get my summers off. During the rest of the year I spend most of my time planning what my students will be doing in school and when they are done we can check it off. Sometimes behavior issues come up or there is a change in schedule where I have no control of so I have to adjust. But with the summer I can do whatever I please. Sometimes that is more stressful for me because I don't know where to start. I have to come up with a game plan and execute it every day because the clock doesn't stop when we want it to. James 4:14 tells us not to worry about tomorrow. I'll end with Matthew 6: 25-34 from the Message it expands on the same sentiments:

'If you decide for God, living a life of God-worship, it follows that you don't fuss about what's on the table at mealtimes or whether the clothes in your closet are in fashion. T here is far more to your life than the food you put in your stomach, more to your outer appearance than the clothes you hang on your body. Look at the birds, free and unfettered, not tied down to a job description, careless in the care of God. And you count far more to him than birds. Has anyone by fussing in front of the mirror ever gotten taller by so much as an inch? All this time and money wasted on fashion—do you think it makes that much difference? Instead of looking at the fashions, walk out into the fields and look at the wildflowers. They never primp or shop, but have you ever seen color and design quite like it? The ten best-dressed men and women in the country look shabby alongside them. If God gives such attention to the appearance of wildflowers—most of which are never even seen—don't you think He'll attend to you, take pride in you, do His best for you? What I'm trying to do here is to get you to relax, to not be so preoccupied with getting, so you can respond to God's giving. People who don't know God and the way He works fuss over these things, but you know both God and how He works. Steep your life in God-reality, God-initiative, God-provisions. Don't worry about missing out. You'll find all your everyday human concerns will be met. Give your entire attention to what God is doing right now, and don't get worked up about what may or may not happen tomorrow. God will help you deal with whatever hard things come up when the time comes.

What adjustments can you make to your schedule?

Do you feel like you are overwhelmed and worried?

Do you feel like you are lazy and lethargic?

1. **Psalms 20:4**- God wants to give you your desires and make your plans succeed.

2. **Psalms 33:11**- The Lord's plans stay firm and will last forever.

3. **Proverbs 12:5**- The plans of the righteous are just, but the advice of the wicked is deceitful. We need to get advice from spiritual people.

4. **Proverbs 21:5**- The plans of the diligent lead to profit as surely as haste leads to poverty.

5. **Genesis 7:16**- We just need to trust God with our plans. Noah had no choice but to trust that these animals were going to come in two by two because he really could not do much about it.

6. **2 Corinthians 6:4-10** Life has its ups and downs but we can still live a godly life.

7. **Nehemiah 9:19-35** –God was patient but they didn't listen. He does His part we need to do ours.

Pray: That God will give you wisdom to make the best choices.

Work

Be Excellent

Your calling is calling you...Monster.com

Do Work! ...Christopher Big Black Boyken

The Best part of waking up ...Folgers

Be great- ...Powerbar

There are no whites working at GE no blacks either, just people and we need more ...GE

The passionate pursuit of perfection ...Lexus

I'd rather die of thirst than drink a cup of mediocrity ...Stella Artois

Colossians 3:23 is the theme scripture for this chapter. This scripture tells us that we are working for the Lord. Anything we do we are working for God. Christians should always be the best workers on their jobs because they have the best boss. Obviously everyone is in a different situation. There are Christians out there who are definitely in the wrong jobs and need to quit and find something else quickly. Others of you will just complain wherever it is you go.

Some people make me laugh when they say I am being persecuted because I am a Christian. No, you are getting persecuted because you are selfish and lazy. Do not get the grace stuff twisted and take advantage of it. Jesus came to serve, He was a hard worker. Now you probably will get persecuted if you are trying to be righteous but things are very different these days. So you could easily do a good job while living at peace with everyone. (Hebrews 12:14)

The Bible gives us many good scriptures on working. 2 Thessalonians 3: 10 tells us if we don't work we don't eat. 1 Timothy 5: 18 says, a worker deserve his wages. It is important to work. The Bible says, *If a man does not work he does not eat... and...We need to work for our wages.* We recently had to have a big meeting at church to decide or revisit what benevolence is for. It is not for someone who has fallen on hard times. We can't use our church benevolence for someone who is late on rent. Times are difficult for all of us; we have to live within our means.

Camp is coming up. Ever since I came to this church, camp has been the last week of August and it cost around $300. Camp is an awesome experience for teens and preteens to grow spiritually. Every year someone comes up right before the deadline saying that they don't have enough money for camp. I tried to help this year by selling water. I made $200 in two Sundays. Not bad. The point of this story is that there is always a way to make money. Even in hard times.

Proverbs 31 tells us how hard women worked. Yes, men lead the house but the women of the Bible were strong; they figured stuff out. They made money by selling things on the side and they worked extra hard to take care of the family. I am grateful for my wife because she is able to figure things out. She is now staying at home with our daughter but she is still able to work out of the house and bring in extra income.

Now let's remember that Jesus is still Lord. Work is not Lord. Don't let work get in the way of your life. We just talked about not doing too much. It is great to make a lot of money but you need to remember you are a Christian. God takes care of your needs.

Remember, whatever you do, do it as if you were working for the Lord. How do you feel when you wake up in the morning getting ready for your day? Do you feel the way those advertisers describe their product in the slogans? You should also enjoy your job. There is no perfect job out there, so you have to learn how to be content. That doesn't mean settle for junk, always try to be your best. The same goes with school.

It is so easy these days to be deceitful at work, but as Christians we know we need to have integrity. Little white lies, punching in different hours, making excuses for yourself are sometimes the norm in certain workplaces but again as Christians we cannot compromise.

It is so easy to gossip or slander people at work. You can call it water cooler talk. You can flirt with you co-workers and justify it by saying everyone else is doing it. When I was single and working, some people thought I was gay (not happy) because I would not talk about women.

Now it is natural to notice a beautiful woman or handsome guy, but most conversations at work usually have a lot more to do with lust than just noticing. We have to be set apart, we have to be Holy. We are different and that will be weird to people. We don't curse and when people do they should feel uncomfortable around us.

I have been teaching for about nine years now. The biggest thing these kids are lacking now is positive role models. Many teachers that I work with curse, smoke, lie, steal, get drunk, have premarital sex, and the list goes on. It breaks my heart to see that. It is basically tells these kids it is all right to do these things. It is hard to have any hope for these kids. I hate to say that, but the kids in this society have so much against them.

We need to stand up tall at our jobs no matter what you do. Whatever you do, do it great. There are so many people who just don't care, don't be one of them. If you are a student, be the best student you can be. If you are a custodian, clean like your supervisor was watching your every move. If you are a supervisor, treat the workers the way you would want them to treat your mother. We don't work for men, we work for God.

God has allowed certain authority to be in place so we can grow from it. Take the opportunity to be like Christ wherever you are. Hopefully you can help someone become a Christian.

I want to end with Luke 16 the parable of the shrewd manager. If you can be trusted with a lot now maybe you could be trusted with more later. There are three big parts to this. First, Jesus tells us the parable. Then He explains the parable. Then He ends up by telling us not to serve both God and mammon.

First the parable, it is about some guy in a tough situation, then he figures something out to make money. It may seem weird but he made it happen. Jesus always used stories to give us examples.

Then the explanation, it says use your worldly wealth to gain friends. What does that mean? If you can not be trusted with worldly wealth you cannot be trusted with true riches. If you cannot be trusted with others' stuff, should you get you own stuff? God uses our jobs to test how well we can take care of other things.

Finally, He says serve God not mammon. What's mammon? The NIV version calls it money, but that's not exactly what it was saying. It is a worldly gain or a greedy pursuit. Money is not bad. It is the greedy, worldly pursuit of money. So let's be grateful that God allows is to grow and learn from different situations. Jesus is Lord and He will take care of you. It is a privilege and honor to work for Him.

Do you love your job?

Is God using you at your job?

What would your boss say about your work performance?

1. **Genesis 2:15-** From the beginning man worked the land. It is normal to work.

2. **Genesis 31:41-** Jacob worked with all his strength for 20 years and he did not even have a retirement plan.

3. **Numbers 7:5-** A man's work is give and take. One does something for someone else's good.

4. **2 Chronicles 31:21-** Work wholeheartedly and you will prosper. When you give your heart to anything you will usually get results.

5. **Ecclesiastes 2:10-** Delight in your work. It doesn't help when you complain about your job every day.

6. **1 Corinthians 9:6-** Barnabas and Paul worked for a living. It is possible to be very effective in ministry and still have a secular job.

7. **Colossians 3:12-** Therefore, as God's chosen people, holy and dearly loved, clothe yourselves with compassion, kindness, humility, gentleness and patience. Put these clothes on when you leave for work every morning.

Pray: That you will be great at what ever you do.

Work out

Take care of the Temple

It keeps going and going...Energizer

Good to the last Drop...Maxwell coffee

Power to push... Power bar

The power to be your best...Apple

Change your body change your life... Gold's Gym

Better....New York sports Club

You can have a body like mine ...Charles Atlas

As Christians, our lives have to be impressive to people, and part of that is our physical appearance. In Genesis we are told that we were made in God's image. I simply can not imagine God as an unhealthy, overweight man, nor can I see Jesus, the carpenter, as fat, unfit, and weak. If I offend you, sorry, but most of us need to make improvement with our physical beings and most of us can. We just choose not to. I understand that there are people out there with specific medical issues beyond their control but God has allowed these situations for specific reasons. I know someone who was paralyzed in a car accident, is in a wheelchair, and is still in great shape. We are without excuse!

I'm six feet tall and 155 pounds. I still fit in the same clothes I had from high school. I try so hard to gain weight with no results. The more I eat, the more that comes out of the other end. I know people, who have the opposite problem, but I don't want you to compare yourself to me and I am not comparing myself to you. The goal is to take care of God's temple, so that you can be your best for Him.

Some of us made tragic health choices like abusing drugs and alcohol that were detrimental to our health prior to becoming Christians. Others taint out bodies by not considering the types of foods that we are consuming. We have to pick the right foods to eat. I am not big on any sort of diet except as necessary for those with specific health issues. Eating organic, Atkins, red meat, green eggs and ham, or whatever the latest fad is, is a personal decision. I do believe in a balanced diet. God made everything good for us to eat; we just have to avoid all extremes. I am Italian and we eat a lot of pasta and red meat and a lot of other things that are considered to be bad for you, by paternal grandparents recently passed away in their 90s, and they enjoyed their share of pasta. My mother's parents are still living and they are more active than many people my age. My Nanni says she stays young by working hard and eating well.

Now I am not talking about looking like the super model image the world portrays as healthy. There are many people who won't eat certain things when God declared it fine to eat. (Mark 7:19) It is fine to be a vegetarian or be on a special diet, but don't make others struggle by making them oversensitive to your preferences (1 Corinthians 8:13). We need to be concerned primarily with eating and exercising in a way that positively impacts our health. Don't become consumed with your outward appearance either. Avoid all extremes. (Ecclesiastes 7:18). Eat in good conscience and good health. Make the most of your time and ability and just shake what your Heavenly Father gave you.

I don't want this chapter to make you struggle. I want you to be inspired to worship God with your body. All of us could make improvements in this area. Just like everything else we have to be spiritual about the choices we make.

For the second part of this chapter I want to look at some mighty men of the Bible. I don't want you to look at these guys and get inspired to kill people. I just want you to see how they used their bodies to serve God.

Just look at David from the story of David and Goliath in 1 Samuel 17. He was just a young a boy and he was not afraid to sacrifice his body for God. Goliath was said to be nine feet tall. That's pretty "Gianormous". So it's not about how big you are it's about using your body as a living sacrifice. (Romans 12:1)

In 1 Chronicles 11: 10-25 and 2 Samuel 23:8-23 we get the story of David's mighty men. There are a few crazy stories about them and they are described by name. Sam Laing does a great job describing them in his book Mighty Man of God. These are some of David's mighty men:

Josheb raised his spear against eight hundred men, whom he killed in one encounter.

Eleazar stood his ground and struck down the Philistines till his hand grew tired and froze to the sword.

Shammah took his stand in the middle of the field. He defended it and struck the Philistines down, and the LORD brought about a great victory.

Then when David longed for water and said, "Oh, that someone would get me a drink of water from the well near the gate of Bethlehem!" The three mighty men broke through the Philistine lines, drew water from the well near the gate of Bethlehem and carried it back to David.

Such were the exploits of the three mighty men.

Abishai raised his spear against three hundred men, whom he killed. He became their commander, even though he was not included among them.

Benaiah was a valiant soldier who performed great exploits. He struck down two of Moab's best men. He also went down into a pit on a snowy day and killed a lion. And he struck down a huge Egyptian. Although the Egyptian had a spear in his hand, Benaiah went against him with a club. He snatched the spear from the Egyptian's hand and killed him with his own spear. Such were the exploits of Benaiah, son of Jehoiada; he too was as famous as the three mighty men. He was held in greater honor than any of the Thirty, but he was not included among the Three. And David put him in charge of his bodyguards.

These guys were fired up. I love the story of how the three guys attacked the Philistines just to get a cup of water. That is a great amount of loyalty, dedication, and hard work for something that seems so small. Health may seem like a small part of discipleship but we can't forget the small parts, as they are all important.

I want to end with Joshua 14:10-12 "Now then, just as the LORD promised, he has kept me alive for forty-five years since the time he said this to Moses, while Israel moved about in the desert. So here I am today, eighty-five years old! I am still as strong today as the day Moses sent me out; I'm just as vigorous to go out to battle now as I was then." No matter how old you are or whatever your condition is you can still be fired up for God. Strive to live a life that will inspire people. Joshua did 45 years of ministry and at 85 years old he said, "I am as strong as I was when I was 40." What is your life telling others?

Are you in good shape?

What can you do to be healthier?

Are you obsessive with anything?

1. **1 Corinthians 3: 16-17-** You are God's sacred temple. He allows His Holy Spirit to live in you.

2. **1 Corinthians 6: 19- 20-** Our body is not ours, so we need to honor God with our body.

3. **Psalm 73: 3-5-** We do not need to compare our selves to non believers. Don't be jealous of them. Our goal is not to have a perfect body.

4. **Proverbs 31: 17-** The Bible even tells us that the women's arms were strong.

5. **Ephesians 6: 10-** Our primary strength has to come from God. He will make us spiritually and physically strong.

6. **1 John 2: 14-** "I write to you because you are strong." There is a confidence in being strong.

7. **3 John 2-** There is a lot more you can do when you are healthy, so enjoy good health.

Pray: That God will help you to be in the best health possible.

Eat

Hospitality and Evangelism

Breakfast of champions... Wheaties

Billions and billions served... Mc Donald's

There's a smile in every Hershey's bar... Hershey's

Have a coke and a smile... Coke

Finger licking good...KFC

Their Magically Delicious... Lucky Charms

MMM MMM Good..... Campbell

Every year our church has a marriage retreat to help couples in the church grow closer to one another and to grow closer to God. Last year my wife and I had the privilege and honor to teach one of the classes. The topic given to us was "Hospitality and Evangelism". I had to ask a lot of questions about what I should be doing for the class. Is it about hospitality or is it about evangelism? I basically figured out it was about both and then it started to make sense. They go hand and hand. Then I came up with a title for the class: "Come join our Family".

Well, I thought it was a nifty title because as a Christian married couple that should be our invitation to everyone else. Children, teens, campus students, singles and all other Christians should feel comfortable coming to our house. Even if you are not married you should make your house available. I remember when I was studying the Bible to become a Christian this brother, Yunior, invited me to sleep over his house. I was blown away by the offer, even though I couldn't sleep because I thought my car was going to get broken into and I was awakened by a rooster at the crack of dawn. I was impressed by the hospitality. We later became roommates and our household became the place where other single brothers could crash. Even though there were already five of us living there, we always had room.

Why do we do that? Because God has blessed us. What we have is not our own. It is also good for our hearts when we have others over. The Bible also says that they will know we are disciples by our love. (John 13:35) The best way to help people get to know Jesus is through love and one of the best ways to show love is by feeding someone.

We just had some friends over the other night. They moved out of town and they were in New York for a week. We cooked them a nice dinner on short notice and had a great time of fellowship. They are not interested in studying the Bible right now and we didn't force that thought down their throat, but they know we are available if they wanted to. The Bible says plant the seed, water it and God will make it grow. (1 Corinthians 3:6) We just have to do our part and God will do His.

I can't count how many people I have invited to church but I know the number that have accepted my invitation have been much fewer than the ones I invited. God had a great banquet and invited people. (Luke 14:16) They gave a bunch of excuses and He invited more and even some of those weren't ready. God wants us to eat with Him and enjoy His favor. We should have the same heart towards people. I know my main purpose to invite anyone out to anything is so they could draw closer to God. If I get rejected, I have to understand that they are rejecting God. (John 15:18)

Don't be discouraged if someone does not accept your invitation. Don't be shocked if you eat with someone and they disagree with you about your belief in God. We don't need to convert anyone to our beliefs anyway. Just work on loving people sincerely from the heart. We can all work on that. It takes a lot out of you when you plan something and people don't come. Or when you serve someone and they are ungrateful. It is tough to show unconditional love. But that is what Jesus did for us.

This is a new era in our Christian walk. Everybody has heard of Jesus. There is some kind of church wherever you go. People say God Bless you all the time, even when you sneeze. With all of this people are more deceived and more sinful than ever. When we say God Bless you, it has no meaning now. You can't just invite people out to church and you can't just mention Jesus. You have to be about Jesus.

Many times in the Bible we see Jesus reclining with people at the dinner table and people would get mad at Him because He would eat with sinners. I love how He responded, "It is not the well who need a doctor but the sick." (Mark 2:16-17) Jesus wasn't embarrassed to eat with anyone because He knew He was doing it to help people get to heaven.

Jesus just liked to eat too. Even when He comes back from the dead He talks about eating some fish. (Luke 24:41) I'm sure it was great to hang out with Jesus but I'm sure He was very focused too. His conversations must have been seasoned with salt (Colossians 4:6) Again we must imitate this stuff. We need to bring back some hot sauce in our lives. People need to feel the heat with a whole lot of love. When there is love in the room it brings a whole lot of fire.

Christians need to be more passionate about what we have in Christ. Way too many conversations have not been Spirit filled. People are excited about Transformers, worried about the economy, but not really concerned about salvation. In a way it has become weird to speak about spiritual topics. It made some people feel uncomfortable, so we tried to be more relatable. Now we are just straight up flirting with the world.

I heard this poem a few times that says, "I'll have three dollars worth of God please." I'm not sure who wrote it but it is a good description of some Christians today. That's where we are at and I don't think we notice it. Nobody wants to be bothered. No one wants to rustle feathers. They'll just take three dollars worth of God. They'll show up. They'll do this or that if they are told to do it, just as long as it's only three dollars worth. This has got to change.

We need to be inviting people over constantly. Eat with sinners. I am totally for being wise. Don't invite a pedophile over your house and leave them alone with your daughter. Do not invite friends over and shout at them all night, telling them that they are going to hell. Be wise. But don't be afraid of everyone and everything. The same God who brought the Israelites out of Egypt will protect you.

Take some time out to plan a day when you could serve someone. Take a brother out to eat. Have the couple from out of town sleep over and make them an omelet in the morning. Invite a non-Christian over your house for dinner. Do something to be out of yourself. Just take some time out to eat, drink and be merry with someone else and hopefully they will draw closer to God.

When will you have someone over?

What else can you do to encourage others?

Are people glad to invite you over?

1. **1 Peter 4:9-** Offer hospitality to one another without grumbling. It needs to be an enjoyable thing.

2. **Colossians 4:2-6-** Pray that God will open the door and that you can use your conversations with outsiders to encourage them.

3. **1 Thessalonians 1:2-10-** The church is thankful when you love and serve. It sets an example for others.

4. **3 John 8-** Show hospitality to people who are working hard for the Lord.

5. **1 Timothy 5:10-** We should be known for good deeds such as hospitality, bringing up kids, washing feet and helping those in trouble.

6 **Acts 28:7-** We can entertain for more than one day. Open your home to some out- of-towners.

7. **Romans 12:13-** The Bible tells us to "Practice" hospitality because the more we do it the better we get at it.

Pray: That you can use your life to be evangelistic.

Drink

Bad company corrupts good character

Guinness is good for you... Guinness

Honor thy self ...Johnnie Walker

Just what the doctor ordered .... L & M cigarettes

Obey your thirst... Sprite

Blow some my way.... Chesterfield Cigarettes

Experience is the best teacher.... In choosing a cigarette your T-zone will tell you why more doctors smoke camels than any other cigarette.... Camel

It's all about the beer....Heineken

Stay Thirsty My Friends... Dos Equis

I'm sure you have heard of the saying being in the wrong place at the wrong time. For this chapter we are going to talk about being in the right place at the right time. I am sure many of us are guilty of the prior. Even if it is the neighborhood we grew up in. People, places and things influence how we behave. The Bible says it well "Bad company corrupts good character".(1 Corinthians 15:33) These principles along with many others are implemented in the Chemical Recovery group in my church. We call it CR.

I am not going to give you a detailed history of the group. I am just going to steal some ideas to help with this chapter. CR was started because someone realized that people who were addicted to a substance before they became a Christian, had different issues then someone who wasn't. At one point people couldn't relate or understand why the Holy Spirit wasn't enough for everyone. Now don't get me wrong, the Holy Spirit is always enough. The thing is we don't understand it enough.

Drugs and alcohol destroy brain cells. So when you abuse a substance you do things a "normal" person wouldn't do. Then those things also have an effect on how you live today. The same way we would communicate differently with a young child or an adult that has the mind of a child, we need to try a different approach with these different situations. I have heard people say your emotions get locked up at the age you first started using drugs. So if you started smoking cigarettes at 10 years old, emotionally you will act like a 10 year old. That's a scary thing, a 40 year old with 10-year old emotions, but is it very true.

But what if you never used drugs? Amen, you saved your self from a lot of pain, but we all need to be sensitive to this. Even if you never used drugs I could guarantee that most of you were addicted to something else at one point. Even though it may not be the same, it is similar in many ways. Addictions to pornography, eating, TV, video games, gambling, stealing, or anything else that became your idol at one point can be considered an addiction. Even people who say I can not function without a cup of coffee; that is an addiction. The only thing you should be addicted to is God.

But now we are Christians. We don't do the things we used to do anymore or maybe not as much. So what is all of this about? Why do we need a CR ministry? Because all of these things develop bad habits and we have to relearn good habits. Even if you are not doing the same habits, it is going to take years to purify your mind. I was never addicted to drugs or alcohol myself but my mind is polluted with plenty of other things. I know for me just being around drugs and alcohol will take my mind to nasty places.

Drugs and alcohol usually lead to sex, violence, vulgar language, theft, pain, and death. So now, if I watch a violent movie, it will take my mind back to those places. We will talk more about where God wants our mind to be in the next chapter. There are limits to things. Everything is permissible but not everything is beneficial (1 Corinthians 10:23) It is not sin to have a drink. Jesus drank wine, He even made wine. (John 2:1) The Bible even says a little wine is good (1 Timothy 5:23) But if that little bit takes you places where you know you shouldn't be that little bit is no good. You need to make wise decisions for you to work out your own salvation with fear and trembling (Philippians 2:12)

The CR ministry is based on the 12 steps set up by AA. This list doesn't just pertain to Alcohol. It can pertain to any sin in our life. These are the original Twelve Steps as published by Alcoholics Anonymous.

1. We admitted we were powerless over alcohol—that our lives had become unmanageable.

2. Came to believe that a Power greater than ourselves could restore us to sanity.

3. Made a decision to turn our will and our lives over to the care of God as we understood Him.

4. Made a searching and fearless moral inventory of ourselves.

5. Admitted to God, to ourselves, and to another human being the exact nature of our wrongs.

6. Were entirely ready to have God remove all these defects of character.

7. Humbly asked Him to remove our shortcomings.

8. Made a list of all persons we had harmed, and became willing to make amends to them all.

9. Made direct amends to such people wherever possible, except when to do so would injure them or others.

10.Continued to take personal inventory and when we were wrong promptly admitted it.

11.Sought through prayer and meditation to improve our conscious contact with God as we understood Him, praying only for knowledge of His Will for us and the power to carry that out.

12.Having had a spiritual awakening as the result of these steps, we tried to carry this message to alcoholics, and to practice these principles in all our affairs.

I think every sinner saved by grace should think about this list daily and keep their sin in the forefront of their mind. We need to stay humble so we stay as far away from sin as possible. We can't go to the same places we used to go to, we can't hang out with the same people we used to. We need to live a new life. We need to be at the right places at the right time.

This is a prayer that is said at the end of all AA meetings and that I have posted outside my door. "God grant me the serenity to accept the things I cannot change and the courage to change the things I can and the wisdom to know the difference." We all have shortcomings. Many of them are things we can change, for the rest we just trust it to God. Make the best decision you can to be around the right people in the right places at the right times.

Did you admit to yourself that you are powerless over sin?

Do you try to protect yourself and others from falling into temptation?

What are some places or activities you need to avoid?

1. **Genesis 9: 21-** Moses became drunk and he lay naked. Getting drunk causes moral laxity.

2. **Proverbs 23: 20-21-** Don't hang out with drunkards. That is no benefit to you or them.

3. **Isaiah 19: 14-** Drinking makes you dizzy. It makes you stager around your vomit.

4. **Job 15:34-** The company of the godless will be barren. To some people it may seem like the only way to make friends is by getting drunk with them.

5. **Psalm 14:5-** God is present in the company of the righteous. I would rather be righteous and hang out with God.

6. **Proverbs 21:16-** A man who strays from the path of understanding comes to rest in the company of the dead. Don't be foolish, stay safe.

7. **Jeremiah 15:17-** I never sat in the company of revelers, never made merry with them; I sat alone because your hand was on me and you had filled me with indignation.

Pray: That God will keep you away from bad company.

Be merry

Do not be depressed or discouraged

The best a man can get...Gillette

Progress is our most important products...GE

I'm lovin' it....McDonald's

Because I'm worth it.... L'Oreal

A mind is a terrible thing to waste... United Negro college Fund

Be all that you can be... Army

Be Happy ....Clinique

What a day to continue working on this chapter. I had to pick up my mother from the airport at 1:00 in the morning because her flight was delayed. Then I was woken up in the morning by a call about a situation with the pre-teen ministry. My wife is missing one hundred dollars she left in the daycare. Then a brother who promised me three hundred dollars said he still didn't have it. My wife's hair appointment got canceled. I had to give someone $200 last minute. My wife waited in another hair salon for 30 minutes and the beautician didn't show up. I just went to pick her up to bring her to another salon. I hit two big potholes. I got a huge scratch on my arm from I don't know where, and now I have a headache.

The Bible says Rejoice in the Lord always. I'll say it again: Rejoice! (Philippians 4:4)I guess it was a great time to work on rejoicing always. It is easy to rejoice when things are going great but not so easy when you are annoyed every five minutes by something new. Is it possible to rejoice always? It must be, the Bible says it twice. I was annoyed a lot this morning. But I knew I was working on this chapter. So it forced me even more to brush off the negative feelings and think about things that are lovely. The times I stepped into my car I put on my Christian CD. When you listen to songs like, "His Grace is Enough," it is hard to get upset.

I struggle with depression so this is not always easy for me. I saw a few different therapists and they all say something different. I think most of them are just trying to make money. One therapist told me, "You have a job, you have a beautiful wife, friends to talk to, and a God to pray to. You will be fine." I feel like that was the best advice I ever got from any session. Bottom line it is a decision to rejoice.

Sometimes I enjoy being down and moody. I used to love to listen to crazy music with lyrics about how the world was so messed up. I spent many years filling my head with negative thoughts. So now I have to work to fill them with positive thoughts. I have to watch my tongue because my first reaction to many things is a complaint. I complain about how people drive. I complain about how people raise their kids. I complain about how people dress. I complain about whatever I feel like complaining about, but that's not good for my spirit or my soul or for others.

Let's look at a few great men of the Bible who got down and depressed. We can start with Adam the first man, he lived in paradise but he ate one fruit and he gets kicked out forever. That's a bummer. Cain was depressed because of sin. He didn't know what to do with himself. (Gen 4.6-7). Abraham felt down (Gen 15) Jonah was depressed (Jonah 4). Elijah struggled (1 Kings 19). King Saul had issues (1 Sam 16). Jeremiah and Job had some rough times through out their whole books. David was down a few times through the Psalms (38: 6,8) but he always repented.

The Bible does tell us to mourn but we can even rejoice in our suffering. You don't need to laugh when someone dies but we can be grateful for their life. We shouldn't be fired up to get into a car accident but we should be grateful it wasn't more serious. There are many other sad examples but we can't allow them to ruin our day.

The Bible also says to give thanks (1 Thessalonians 5:18). We can do that because we hope in God (Ps 42:5). We need to be like Paul, he knew how to find pleasure in little or much. (Philippians 4:12) Maybe you just need a hobby to get your mind off of things. You can sing like Saul (1 Sam 16:14-23) it takes away the evil spirits

While I was searching for more help with this topic, I found some good information at Christiananswers.net. There were six pointers they gave about handling depression. 1. Avoid being alone. 2. Seek help from others. 3. Sing. 4. Praise and give thanks. 5. Lean on the power of God's Word. 6. Rest in God's Spirit. There were a few other pointer that I got on this website that I feel were helpful. Paul Taylor of Eden Communications shares some common sense suggestions for those weighed down by fear, anxiety, worry, etc...

1. It could be the guilt from the sin in your life. 2. It could be sleep. Humans generally need eight to nine hours. 3. You may need to be more realistic. One day at a time. 4. Listen to some calming music. 5. Have fun, get your mind off your fears and worries. 6. Talk to someone, let it out. You don't want to explode. 7. Take action. The more you procrastinate the deeper it will get. 8. Exercise. Medical studies show this reduces anxiety. 9. Professional Help. If needed seek out a professional 10. I added write a prayer journal. It is good to see your thoughts.

Many of these seem like common sense, but we usually don't do the things we know are right. Depression and discouragement just like any other sin have to be worked on. It may seem more difficult and there will be different ways to encourage others but you still need to repent.

As I was researching ways to treat depression I found some of the causes of depression. There are eight causes of depression according to Gary Collins Christian Counseling. 1. Biological factors, 2. learned helplessness, 3. parental rejection, 4. abuse, 5. negative thinking, 6. life stress, 7. anger, and 8. guilt. If you know the cause of the issues you can better treat it.

Hopefully looking at all of these pointers gives you some ammunition to better fight off your discouragement because no matter how deep your struggles are you have to work on it. You can not allow your life to revolve around your emotions. You need to have faith that you can change. You need to get help from people and you need to help people. Sin is a scary thing; it can take you to scary places. The last thing I would want is someone to read this book and get guilted out and commit suicide.

When we are trying to help others we need to be careful we don't treat any two people the same. Some people will respond by just repenting and moving on. If you use the same words in a certain tone with someone else, it might take them even further back a few steps. Like any time you are going to interact with people pray for a lot of wisdom and do everything out of love.

God loves you and He does not want you to be bound by the sin of depression any more. Satan knows how much you are worth so he is trying to keep you bound as long as he can. Fight the devil off and rejoice.

What is the cause of your discouragement?

How do you stay encouraged?

How do you encourage others?

1. **2 Corinthians 4:8-9, 16-18** - We are hard pressed on every side but not crushed.

2. **1 Peter 5:6-7** - God tells us to cast our anxieties on Him because He cares for us.

3. **Romans 15:13** - The God of hope will fill you with joy and peace as you trust in Him.

4. **Proverbs 12:25** - An anxious heart weighs down; kind words cheer up. Let's encourage one another.

5. **Romans 8:26-28** - The Spirit will help us in our weakness even when we don't know how to pray.

6. **Hebrews 13:6** - "The Lord is my helper; I will not be afraid." There are certain things we just have to remember and repeat over and over.

7. **2 Thessalonians 2:16-17** - God will give us eternal encouragement. Just stick in there buddy.

Pray: For all the things you are gratefully for and to live a life of gratitude.

Reflect

How are you doing?

1. How consistent have you been? **A** Reading and studying every day. **B** Getting in the bare minimum reading. **C** Inconsistent reading. **D** Not reading (you probably wouldn't be at this point)

2. How are you feeling? **A** Excited and growing. **B** At least I made it to this point. **C** This is not great so far why should I continue. **D** I hate this book

3. What are you learning? **A** I am drawing closer to God. **B** Some things in here are cool. **C** It's not really clicking so far but I hope it will. **D** I am doing worse than when I started.

4. How is your relationship with God? **A** I think about Him more. **B** I guess it's ok. **C** I'm trying but it's too hard. **D** It's not good at all.

5. How is your prayer time? **A** I am praying more. **B** It's fine. **C** I pray. **D** I don't pray much.

6. How do you view Jesus? **A** I am eternally grateful for His sacrifice, He is my Lord and Savior. **B** He is a good example. **C** He seems interesting. **D** He was not cool.

7. How are your relationships? **A** I tried some things and they are getting better. **B** I see the things I need to work on. **C** I tried my best, other people need to reach out to me. **D** I'm better off alone.

8. What have you changed in your thinking? **A** I changed a few things. **B** I made one change. **C** I am thinking about it. **D** I think I am fine the way I am

9. How have you changed your actions? **A** I am doing things differently. **B** I changed one thing. **C** I haven't done anything but maybe I will. **D** I'm just fine the way I am.

10. How has you attitude changed? **A** The more I learn about God the more I learn how much greater He is than me. **B** I am learning some practical things. **C** I knew this stuff already, nothing has changed. **D** Life stinks and so do these questions.

11. How are you going to end this book? **A** I want to give it my all because I want to draw closer to God. **B** At least I'll be done with it soon. **C** Maybe I will finish it one day. **D** I'm done.

As you answer these questions I want you to reflect on how you are doing. In this chapter I want you to think about where you are in your walk with God. It is cool because Jesus asks a lot of questions in the Bible so I took eleven of them and I thought it made a good chapter to reflect on.

I will start off in Matthew chapter 16 verse 13. Jesus asks, "WHO DO THE PEOPLE SAY THE SON OF MAN IS?" He starts of with a question to everyone. Who do people say I am? How would you answer that question? We mentioned a few things about Him in this book, but one thing I want you to remember is that He is the Goal that we are aiming for. He is also the Way to the Goal that we are trying to achieve.

As we wrap up this book the last seven chapters will be about heaven. Now in seven chapters we will talk a lot about heaven but that is still nowhere close to even giving a slight idea of what it will be like. Think of Jesus being in Heaven. Remember all of the steps He told us to take to get to Heaven and follow them. Then we will be done, our journey will be over, we will have no other steps to take because we reached our goal. We would have made it to the Son.

The next question is in the same story in verse 15 and it adds a little more dimension to the first question. "WHAT ABOUT YOU?" Jesus is not only concerned about what people say. He is concerned about what you say. He doesn't want us to go with the flow of any group. You can't give my answer. He wants us to come with our own convictions. So when Jesus asks you, what about you, what will you say? I hope you will have a good answer.

The third question comes from the previous chapter in verse 16 and it is very blunt. "ARE YOU STILL SO DULL?" That's a tough question. How do you answer that? Can you say yes or no? I don't think so; I just think it is a question of reflection. A question to get you thinking. Why would He ask if you are Dull? Because He wants you to be sharp. So are you sharp? Think about it. Yes, we are going to have our ups and downs, but where do you think God wants us to be. It's obvious. Your walk with God should be making you less dull if you are searching out the Scriptures, faithful in prayer, and humble in your heart.

Then we go to Matthew 20:21 "WHAT IS IT THAT YOU WANT?" Again a very personal question. It is a simple question but a very deep question. What do you want? It is funny how so many people can't answer that question. Sometimes even about simple things like, what to eat or what to wear. But make that a general question and people get really messed up. So I want you to think about it. What do you want from this book? What do you want to look like spiritually 40 days after this? What do you want to be doing in five years? Think about it, what do you want?

Then we go to verse 32 in the same chapter and Jesus says, "WHAT DO YOU WANT ME TO DO?" He wants to help, but we need to know what to ask for. All of these are simple questions but they are very deep. Many people have come to me asking for help, mostly my students at school. They scream out, "I need help!" I ask them what they need help with and they can't answer the question. It sounds weird but many of us do that. Help me. With what? I don't know but I want help.

The reason I can't help someone if they don't know what they want is the same reason why Jesus can't help us if we don't know what we need help with. The question is for us to figure it out. Jesus knows what we need help with. He just wants us to know what we need help with.

Question number six doesn't come from Jesus, it comes from a Pharisee in verse 36. He asks, "WHICH IS THE GREATEST COMANDMENT?" Jesus gives an answer, and it is very important. "Love God with all your mind, soul, heart, and strength. The second is like this, love your neighbor as yourself." If we could put into practice those two simple things the rest would fall into place very easily.

Now that we have some answers and we have some direction, Jesus asks, "WHY ARE YOU AFRAID?" in MARK 4:40 He doesn't want us to be scared, but so many things hold us back. So why are you afraid? What are you afraid of? What is holding you back? Only you can answer those questions. There is something for all of us. Most of us are afraid of failure. I know that is big for me and I have to be honest with myself. When I can confess then I can grow, because I allow Jesus to encourage me not to be afraid.

The next question is one of the main things that hold us back. "DO YOU STILL HAVE NO FAITH?" in MARK4:40. We all struggle with this also. In which situations do you have a lack of faith? What don't you believe God can do? Why? Do you remember that Jesus just said, "Have faith of a mustard seed." A tiny little mustard seed. That's all we need.

The next question is funny. "IF YOU CAN?" in MARK 9:23 It shows lack of faith. Jesus sounds a little sarcastic here. I wonder how He said it. Do you really think I can't do it? Did you not see me multiply two fish for 5,000 people? Did you not see me heal the leper? What about the bleeding woman, the paralytic, Lazarus? I think Jesus can do it.

Question 10 "DO YOU STILL NOT UNDERSTAND?" in MARK 8:21. Most of us still don't. I don't know if we will ever truly understand. Jeremiah 33:3 tells us of things we can't imagine. If we can't imagine it we can't understand it. I think this is talking about the greatness of heaven that we will get into next chapter. But there are some basics things we should understand now.

The last question I want to ask you is the first question that Jesus asks that is recorded in the Bible. It is actually two questions but I will count it as one. "WHY ARE YOU STILL SEARCHING FOR ME?...DIDN'T YOU KNOW I WOULD BE IN MY FATHER'S HOUSE?" (LUKE 2:49) As we are looking for Jesus He reminds us that we don't have to look too far. He hasn't left His father's house.

As you reflect back on all the things in the book don't get overwhelmed. God wants us to be obedient to what we know. If you messed up in one area He forgave you but next time be obedient. Jesus is waiting for you. Look for Him so you can see His glory and get your blessing. Let's reflect on Jesus so we can reflect His Glory.

How did you do on the test?

How's it going now?

Do you need more time?

1. **2 Corinthians 3:18**- When we look at ourselves we should see that our faces reflect the Lord.

2. **Proverbs 27:19**- Water reflects the face and our heart and our mind show who we really are.

3. **1 Corinthians 14:20**- Don't think like children, you are adults you need to figure things out.

4. **2 Peter 3:1-2**- The Bible was written to stimulate thinking. We need to look at the Word and it needs to prompt us to change.

5. **Psalm 7:8**- The psalmist is asking God to judge him according to his righteousness. How would you do on that test?

6. **1 Thessalonians 5:21**- Test everything. We need to make sure things work.

7. **1 John 4:1**- Test the spirits because they all don't come from God. You have to double check your self and you motives all the time.

Pray: That you will be clear minded.

COME

An Invitation to the Banquet

Come and go with me
to my father's house 3x
Come and go with me to my father's house
where there's joy, joy, joy.

There are many rooms
in my father's house 3x
There are many rooms in my father's house
where there's joy, joy, joy.

We're going to have a good time
in my father's house3x
We're going to have a good time in my father's
house
where there's joy, joy, joy.

In a way it must be pretty scary just to be invited somewhere if we don't know what's going on. Come. Where are we going? Jesus says come follow me. (Mark 1:17) All aboard on the ride for eternity. He is calling us daily to get on His bandwagon. We can get on any time before we die and we can make it to our final destination. But we can also decide to get off whenever we please. Some of us will never get on the right train but as long as we are on a train we are going to the place it is leading to. I hope you are not on the wrong train or going in the wrong direction. If you are not sure just look at the map. It has five big letters on it B.I.B.L.E. Those are your basic instructions before leaving earth. ALL ABOARD!

The Bible tells us "No eye has seen, no ear has heard what God has prepared."(1 Corinthians 2:9) It's a faithful ride and we are not faithful people. Or are we? I am riding on the train right now. (I haven't been on the train for a while.) But I don't know who's driving this train. And I am sure 99% of the other riders don't know who is in control either, but we all have faith that we are going to get where we are going. We are not in control. We are going up on skinny stilts, down into the earth, riding with people we have never seen before. That's pretty faithful. We do this stuff all the time. We get on airplanes, we get on roller coasters, we eat food from the Chinese food shops. Everyone responds according to their faith.

In this small world we will encounter many different faiths. God allows the weeds to grow up with the wheat. (Matthew 13:24-30). This might be difficult to understand so Jesus explains it more in verses 36-43. None of us have the perfect plan for this life because none of us are perfect. We all tend to follow someone in some way. The devil wants us to follow his way, but the only way to grow up as wheat is to grow up in the "Way". Jesus is very clear about it: He says He is the "Way". (John 14:6) If we are not part of Jesus' plan then we are part of the problem.

Another parable that is similar is the parable of the nets. (Matthew 13:47) Jesus says He will gather all the fish but He will throw out the bad ones. We are living in a world full of good fish and bad fish. The funny thing is that we were all at one time the bad fish. It is also possible to go back to being that stinky fish. That makes me work hard as a Christian. Even though I know I am not saved by works. I don't want my heart to get hard to I fall from grace.

God's mind is about saving us and it is hard for us to understand. Jesus says He is concerned about the one lost sheep. (Matthew 18:10-14) We look at a broad spectrum of things and God does that also. In looking at and loving everyone He gets deep and personal with every soul. How He does that, I have no idea. People who curse His name, those who call out in bad times and those who pray daily. He knows every individual, personally and He cares and is concerned for your salvation. He has given you His personal invitation. What are you doing with it now?

The invitation lasts. He will not take it back. It is us who deny the invite. He can come at any time to pick us up in His chariot. Will you be ready when He comes?

Jesus is the one who will get us into His kingdom, so we can't kill Him. (Matthew 21:28-32) In the parable of the tenants the Bible tells us that the workers killed the Son. He was only trying to guide them in to His kingdom. Jesus just wants us to follow Him. We have to trust Him.

Don't be jealous either. If God called you earlier or later than someone else, don't worry. (Matthew 20:1-16). Some people won't take the invitation early because of this. Many teens and college students say, "I want to enjoy life first and then become a Christian." Then on the flip side those who got baptized at an early age feel like they missed out on something. Both are wrong. The earlier you accept the invitation the better it is for you. You are not missing out on anything when you choose Jesus early. You are actually gaining a lot more.

This concept applies to many other things. Many people I speak to who did not continue with their education right away are having regrets. It is so much harder to start college or go back to high school when you are older. If you do things right the first time you save a lot of time. I am glad my family forced me to go to college when I did not want to because I was able to get my degrees at an early age and enjoy life now.

John 10 tells us Jesus is the Good Shepherd. He cares about His flock. Jesus knows what is best for us, let's listen to Him and trust His thoughts about us. We are just dumb animals. When we think we know what is best we get into a lot of trouble. I get disturbed when I listen to college students who accept the invitations to all kinds of wild parties. I just heard a group of students who were fired up about an all you can drink party for only five dollars. Those kids are going to get into a bunch of trouble and they don't even know it.

Jesus also talks about separating the sheep and the goats. (Matthew 25:31-46). I hope you can be humble enough to be a sheep. It will be a scary day when Jesus will do His separating. I know there will be plenty of goats who thought they would make it. We are all growing together and God will come at harvest time. (Mark 4:26-29). That can be today. So I don't want to be at the all you can drink party when He comes.

The road is narrow (Matthew 7:13) but I can't even imagine how beautiful it will be at the end of that road. The Bible tells us it is more than we can imagine (Ephesians 3:20) and we can't imagine more than we can imagine. Do you understand that? You can't because it is more than you can imagine. Man, I can't wait to get to this party at the end of this narrow road.

It's a free gift, not even five dollars. Free! Jesus says, "I give you free water" (Revelations 22:17) The water of life is free gift. God wants you to drink of it. Get drunk on God's love. It is the greatest feeling and you can have it with no regrets, just great memories.

Jesus is calling, "I am standing at the door knocking". (Revelations 3: 20) You are invited to the great banquet (Matthew 22:2-14, Luke 14:15-24.) Please accept the invitation. I would force you if I could but God gave you the free choice. You have the invitation, are you coming?

Have you said yes to God's invitation?

Do you understand what you are being invited to?

Are fully committed or would you leave if something better came along?

1. **Isaiah 51:6**-Everything will fall but God's salvation will last forever. Nothing should come before the most important thing.

2. **Jeremiah 23:24**- God is everywhere. He sees what is going on. Why not try to please him?

3. **1 Corinthians 10:26**- Everything belongs to God. Let us be grateful for what He has given us and what He wants to give us in the future.

4. **Philippians 2:10**- Everyone will bow to Jesus in Heaven and on Earth. We know this so let's live accordingly.

5. **1 Peter 4:13**- Even though we suffer now, when Christ's Glory is revealed we will be overjoyed. No Pain, No Gain.

6. **Psalm 19: 1-11**- God's way is the Greatest. Bottom line.

7. **1 John 5:4-5**- Only with Jesus can we overcome the world. He has to be Lord of our lives so we can submit to His will. All He wants to do is shower us with His blessings.

Pray: That God offers you more to life than this

HAVE FUN

Heaven on Earth

Don't you wanna go to that land 3x
where I am bound?
Don't you wanna go that land 3x
where I am bound?

Nothing but love in that land 3x
Where I'm bound.
Nothing but love in that land 3x
Where I am bound.

I've got a savior in that land 3x
Where I am bound
I got a savior in that land
Where I am bound.

What are you binding and what are you loosing? If Heaven is God's throne and the Earth is His footstool, (Isaiah 66:1) what first steps are we taking towards Heaven? Do you remember the famous line by Neil Armstrong? "One small step for man but a giant leap for mankind." It is just like Heaven and Earth. The small steps we take here on earth are going to lead to the giant step we take into eternity. Every step we take here on earth will direct our destiny.

A big part of this chapter is based on Matthew 16:19. If what we bind and loose here on Earth will be bound in Heaven, then what are we binding and loosing? I know for me, one thing I hope for heaven, is that it will be fun. Now it would be pretty dull to live eternity in boredom. I don't know about you but that is one thing that I would not enjoy. That's basically what the word fun means, to enjoy. My hope is to enjoy heaven. So I want to bind that on earth. I want to bind Fun and loose Boredom.

Within all the steps we have talked about so far we did a pretty good job of covering the things God calls us to do on earth. I know you can look at the list of things and say this is not fun, this is burdensome. But Christianity is not burdensome, it is balanced. Some people might say fun is partying all night, getting drunk, or sleeping around. If you party all night you will be tired in the morning, if you get drunk you will have a hangover, if we sleep around we will have shallow relationships or worse get a disease and die.

Let's look at Psalm 16 verse by verse for a minute to see what fun is. 1Keep us safe God, we need you to protect us 2 If we are not with You we will have nothing good 3 We have fun with other Christians 4 You will be guilty if you run after other things than God 5 You give me the right amount of everything 6 Where you tell me to stop is perfect 7 I will praise and worship You 8 Before I do anything I will think, what would Jesus do 9 Then I will be happy and rejoice 10 You will be with me until the day I die11 You showed me the path of life and of eternal pleasures.(My Version)

I think this Chapter of Psalms is chock full of insight into living a fulfilling Christian life. I love verse 6 that says, "His boundaries have fallen in pleasant places." I don't know why but we are a culture that loves to indulge and that's what gets us into trouble. It is funny how we can always be fooled into thinking that what we have is not enough when the Bible says His boundaries stop us at the right places. Our bank accounts tell us when we need to stop spending money. Our stomachs tell us when to stop eating. Our conscience tells us not to steal. But we will still disobey the boundaries that God gives us. Life can be enjoyed without passing them.

Whatever you bind on earth will be bound in Heaven so let's bring good stuff there. I am grateful for that that scripture. I don't want to have the same nonsense in heaven that I had here on earth. I am so grateful for the boundaries. (they have fallen in pleasant places). I am grateful God gets us from the heart. It's a jacked up world, we have impure hearts that get us into trouble but God shows us how not to live that way. We can enjoy life without immorality or drunkenness or debauchery. We can enjoy life to the full. Why does He tell us to be like children? Because they can make a game out of anything. I think my students are nuts but I love when I can see them just start a game with their pencils when they get bored. They don't need the impurities. The idiotic adults introduce the young ones to sin.

Let's enjoy life's simplicity. Look at the clouds. Imagine the faith, the hope that keeps us going. Go to a pet shop, check out some fish or look at some puppies. Laugh with a friend, tell someone you love them, buy your mom a gift, give your wife some flowers, write the minister a thank you card. Go to the beach, climb a mountain, enjoy this beautiful world that God gave us and help someone do the same.

Let's have a blast, guys. Look at David, he danced (2 Sam. 6:14). Now a lot of the dancing we have now is lewd but we don't have to dance in a sexual way. Just get down and move your body in excitement. Think about being around small children. What would be an appropriate way for them to dance? If you are married you can praise the Lord together with your spouse. Marriage is a holy and sacred thing. We talked about it earlier. God made it for us to enjoy.

Shout to the Lord (Psalm 100: 1-15). When was the last time you just shouted as loud as you can, not because you were mad at someone, but with Joy. I dare you to shout right now. If you can't do it right now I challenge you t do it sometime soon. Shout with all your might "I LOVE YOU, LORD!" It's very freeing. Sing loud in the shower. Sing loudly at church. Make up your own words; whatever, man.

Look at (Nehemiah 8:10) God said eat good food, drink sweet drinks, and give some to people who don't have. Then the joy of the Lord will be your strength. There is so much good food to eat in this world and we just get more and more creative in our ways to prepare it. There are so many sweet drinks to consume. Mixing all the different fruits that God had in the Garden of Eden must have been an awesome fruit punch. (could you imagine that they still wanted the one fruit they couldn't have. You probably can.) He also tells us to share with others because it is more fun when you enjoy stuff with others.

Let's remember Jesus tells us He has all authority of heaven and earth (Matt 28:18.) He is the one we need to follow. Did you ever have a connection to a nice restaurant or someone who could get you a good deal on a hotel? That's a good friend to have. Well, Jesus is the best friend to have. He figured out how to live an awesome life on earth. What do you expect, He helped create it. He can also get you into Heaven free of charge. His Father owns it.

Lastly, we have to remember that flesh doesn't get to Heaven (1 Corinthians 15:50). There will be things in Heaven we really won't understand. When people say I am going to have a huge screen TV and play play-station all day, I think they are a little off. We need to see what Jesus was focused on when He was here because He made it to heaven. He is waiting for us. Start binding and loosing for your eternal life. You may have to redefine your definition of Fun.

Do you enjoy your Christian life?

How can you make it more fun?

If Heaven was the same as your life now would you be happy?

1. **Psalm 70:4**- Shout to God. Have you done it yet? Find the time and place to release your inhibitions and Shout to God with all your strength.

2. **Ezekiel 28: 13**- God gave us Eden to enjoy. God created many wonderful and amazing things He wants us to use to have fun.

3. **Colossians 3:2**- Set your minds on things above. We need to have a spiritual mindset to really enjoy life. If not we will always worry about what we do not have.

4. **2 Peter 3:10-15**- God gives us time on earth, but we don't know when He is coming back, so we need to make the most of our time here.

5. **1 Corinthians 10:23-26**- God gives us everything so be careful how you use the things He gave you.

6. **Genesis 14:19**- He is the Creator of Heaven and Earth. So imagine how much better heaven will be because there is no sin.

7. **Psalms 108:5**- God needs to be exalted over Heaven and Earth. So imagine how great God is.

Pray: That you will experience a glimpse of Heaven today.

RUN

Give it your all

In the morning when you rise
Wipe the sleep out from your eyes
Get down on your knees and pray
Going to the streets today
Run to the fight and hold each other tight 2x

When you're out there on the streets
Don't you get burned by the heat
Lift your eyes up to the sky
Let the Spirit be your guide
Run to the fight and hold each other tight 2x

And now when your day is done
And some souls have been won
Get back on your knees and pray
Thank you Lord for the day
Run to the fight and hold each other tight 2x

Today as I am writing this page it is 8-8-08, the opening ceremony of the Summer Olympics in Beijing. How encouraging it must be to walk in those opening ceremonies. Some countries like the USA walk in with a huge crowd and some countries like Bhutan came in with two people. I am sure whoever was there was extremely excited just to make it to the opening ceremonies.

It has to be super encouraging knowing you are the best in your whole country at what you do. Now you are competing to be the best in the whole world. The thing we see the most is track and field because there are so many different events. But imagine that you are the fastest person in the world. That must be a great feeling but I'm sure the person who won the sprint would not win the cross-country race. They have a totally different build and they train in a totally different way. Just the same way a swimmer would not compete in the javelin or a high jumper would not compete in a wrestling competition.

It is the same for the Christian race. Philippians 3:14 tells us to press on towards the goal which is heaven. There is one goal, to fix your eyes on Jesus. (Hebrews 12:2) Now we are not competing against other Christians. The goal is not to be better than someone else. We are competing against ourselves. We are all running our own race at our own pace. We need to run in such a way to get the prize.

I heard a story about a man who was told to run a long distance race carrying a specific load. He felt how heavy it was and started running. He thought to himself *this is not bad, I can do this. I will win this race.* As he was running he met a man struggling with his load so he offered to help. He said *my burden is not that heavy, I will help you with your load.* As he continued he was getting a little bit tired but when he saw a woman who had an extra heavy load, he thought, *she is suffering more than me, let me help her out.* He then took some of her load. He was running more slowly now and growing tired. He thought, *I didn't think this race would be that difficult.* As he continued and was nearing the end he saw a young boy who had stopped to rest. He went over to the boy and noticed his load. He said to himself, *this is too much for a young boy to carry.* He took half of the boy's load.

Now the man had nearly tripled the size of his load. He was so close to the end but he was so tired. His burden was so heavy. He stopped running and started complaining. *This race is impossible. The burden is too heavy. No one will be able to finish. I quit!* At that moment the judge came out and asked him why he had quit. The man replied, "The race is too difficult and my burden is too heavy." The Judge then responded, "I never told you to carry anyone else's load. They were all given their fair share. You chose to make your own rules and you made the race more difficult for yourself."

Galatians 6 helps explain the moral of the story. It tells us to carry each other's burdens and it also says carry your own load. We do need to be there to help others when they struggle but that does not mean we make their problems ours. It is our race to heaven. Others are running their own race. We can help them along the way but we can't run their race. When we try to make up our own rules we will lose the race.

The kingdom of Heaven is a treasure. (Matthew 13: 44-46). Nothing else compares to it. This is a cool parable because when the person finds the treasure they sell everything for it. That is an awesome way to run. Just for the treasure with no other distractions. Now I think that is nearly impossible these days because there are plenty of other things around. So a way that we can make this practical is to do everything as part of the race. If you are eating, working, talking, watching TV, do it spiritually. That's the purpose of this whole book – to think about everything spiritually.

Check out Matthew 13:31-33. It talks about two things that start small and grow into something huge. As you run you should be growing big. Maybe you are not competitive or very athletic so you never really thought about life as a race. Or maybe you did. What is cool about this is that no matter where you are at or what you are starting with you can be something big. You just need to keep growing.

God also says you will get more if you leave everything (Matthew 19:28-30). We always need to rethink our thinking. We can never think we are good. Just like the disciples who were with Jesus knew they had nothing else without Jesus we need to think in the same way.

I love how Philippians 3:7-8 puts it. Consider everything else rubbish. My vacation is coming to an end and I had a blast but even this vacation is rubbish if I don't win my prize. I want to have a great marriage, send my kids to the best schools, and help people to become Christians. But all of that is rubbish if I don't I don't make it to my goal. All of that stuff is great and I think it is part of getting to my goal. But if I gain the world and lose my soul it is not worth anything. It is rubbish.

We know the scripture about storing up treasures in Heaven, I shared it in Step 27 (Matthew 6), but how often do we put it into practice? Most of us focus so much time on storing up our treasures here that we forget about storing up in heaven. I think some people don't know how to do it. Hopefully the book already gave you some ideas and hopefully as you finish it you will come up with more of your own. When I talk about this book helping you, I mean that it leads you back to the Scriptures and it leads you back to praying. I want everyone who is reading this book to think more about Jesus, His Father, and the Spirit.

God says My Word is a Lamp (Psalm:105). His Bible will guide our path. Follow His word and you will know where to run, and if you get confused read more. Again don't worry about other people and what they are doing or not doing. It is your race that you are running.

The finial thought I will end with is, "I am coming quickly" from Revelations 22:20. If Jesus is coming quickly you need to run with all of your might. Don't fight like a man who is beating the air. Run in such a way to get the prize. (1 Corinthians 9:24). Don't be lazy, don't wait, start running now. I want to see you holding up that gold medal at the last day, but more importantly God wants to see you holding up the medal.

How is your race going?

If you were rewarded for effort would you deserve a gold medal?

In which areas do you need to train more so you could be a better runner?

1. **Proverbs 4:11-15**-God set up a straight path for you to run on. Stay on track and you will be fine.

2. **Proverbs 18:10**- Run to the Lord. He is our Father so He wants us to run to Him like the children that we are.

3. **Isaiah 10: 3**- Who are you running to for help? The Bible asks the question, do you have the answer? We can run to many things. God is the only one who will truly help.

4. **Isaiah 40:31**- If you run with the God Father you will not get tired. He is a great coach.

5. **Galatians 2:2**- Do not run in vain. It would be a horrible thing if you worked so hard but for the wrong reason.

6. **Philippians 2:16**- You will not have to say I ran for nothing. It's a good thing to know you were working for the right reasons.

7. **Hebrews 12:1**- Run the race marked out for you. You are not running anyone else's race you have your own race. Don't worry about what others are doing. Be concerned about what God wants you to do.

Pray: That you will give it your all and God will do the rest.

OVERCOME

Struggles and obstacles

We shall overcome 2x
We shall overcome someday
Oh, deep in my heart
I do believe
We shall overcome someday

The Lord will see us through 2x
The Lord will see us through someday
Oh, deep in my heart
I do believe
The Lord will see us through some day

It's on to Victory 2x
It's on to victory someday
Oh, deep in my heart
I do believe
It's on to victory someday

Have you heard the story of the man who was told to push the huge rock? Well, he had a very wise master and he was one of the best workers in his kingdom. So one day the master gave his servant a new task. The master told him he wanted him to push this huge rock. It seemed like an impossible task for the servant. So he started asking a bunch of questions. Where to? How far? For how long? And why? The master didn't answer any of the questions. He just told him to do as he was told.

He got up next morning and started pushing. He pushed until the master told him to stop. When he looked at the rock and it was still in the same position and he shouted at his master, "This is a waste of time, nothing was accomplished today." The master did not reply, but only told him to do the same thing tomorrow. He was confused and frustrated but he obeyed anyway. He continued the same routine day after day and the rock seemed to move nowhere.

When he seemed to be finally resolved with his new position in the kingdom the master came up to him and told him his job was done. He was perplexed but relieved. He then asked his master one more time, "Why did you assign me to a task I could not accomplish?"

The master then told him, "Look at your arms and shoulders, look at your legs, feel the calluses on your hands. You are stronger, more patient, and more disciplined than you have ever been. Now you are ready for the new task that I have prepared for you."

I think this is a great story. I'm sure it is from a sermon I heard somewhere down the line. I don't know where it came from but I will always remember the moral of the story. Sometimes we are going through things and we just have no idea what it is and what we are supposed to be learning from it but God knows. He never gives us more than we can bear. He is the Great Rabbi, the great teacher, so He is always teaching us lessons that prepare us for something greater.

Matthew 19:26 and Mark 10:27 tells us that all things are possible. That could be good or bad. If anything is possible it means it is possible that we fall from grace. That is not the good possibility. The good possibility is Romans 8:28 that all things will work out for good.

The men in our church recently had a service where we talked about a brother who was disfellowshiped. The scripture in Hebrews 12:6 was shared that God disciplines those whom He loves. This brother took God's disciplining lightly which Hebrews 12 also warns against. The result was we could no longer call him our brother. What is the purpose of him not being allowed to fellowship? So he will overcome his sin and turn to repentance.

God's discipline us so that we can grow stronger. He sees our struggles and He cares. He never gives out free handouts, as that doesn't help anyone in the long run. He gives out Life- Lessons that will last with us forever. As we read about these next three stories we see God doesn't want us to jump through hoops either. He loves us and He wants to see us overcome one day at a time.

I wanted to spend the last part of this chapter focusing on Luke chapter fifteen because Jesus tells three stories about the lost in this chapter. I thought I could dedicate half of this chapter to that thought. So we have to look at Luke fifteen to see what we are talking about. There are three parables. The Lost Sheep, The Lost Coin, and The Lost Son. If something is lost that means it belonged somewhere at some point. The place we all belong is with God. So when we stray away from that we are lost. There is a common theme between all of the parables. God rejoices over just one sinner who repents, one sinner who overcomes the obstacles and makes it back to God, because that's the goal.

Part one is the Lost Sheep. We already discussed that Jesus is the good Shepherd, so that makes us His sheep. I'm sure you heard but if you didn't a herd of sheep are a bunch of dumb animals. So when we see that we are compared to sheep it can be an insult. But one good quality sheep have is that they are obedient and loyal. If a Shepherd led them all off of a mountain they would all jump off. That may also be part of how dumb they are. They are so trusting in their shepherd that they would do anything he said.

The part we are talking about here is the lost sheep. If one out of a hundred wanders off Jesus says He is going to look for him. To have 99% of a lot of things is pretty good. If I got 99% on a test that would be great. If I had 99% off my battery left on this laptop I would be able to write for a long time. If attendance at my school was 99% that would be awesome. But if my wife was unfaithful only one time, that would not be cool. If I lost one of my daughters in the mall I wouldn't be excited about that. Just the same way that God wants 100%. You are important, everything about you is important. God wants you. He is trying to get you back. Are you looking for Him?

Part two is the Lost Coin. The coin that we are talking about in these verses is worth about a day's wages. Now living in today's economy we would probably be freaking out to if we lost a day's pay. But some of us wouldn't even care. In the parable the lady is so excited to find her coin she even invites over her friends to rejoice with her. If someone called me up about a coin they lost I don't know if I would come over for that party. But again this story is just stressing how important we are to God. He spent time working for us. So we all count.

Part three is the Lost Son. We talked about this already so I won't spend too much time with the story. I will just focus on the fact that the father was always supportive of his son. To me that's what sums up all of these stories. That no matter how we feel or what obstacles we have in our way our Father in Heaven is cheering us on.

In the 1992 Barcelona Olympic Games Derek Redmond showed us the heart that overcame struggles and obstacles. During his race he tore his hamstring that caused him to fall to the ground. After that he had no chance of winning the race but he still got up and hobbled towards the finish line. As he was struggling, his father came out of nowhere and they cross the finish line together. Our Father is doing the same for us.

What's in your way?

How do you cope with the obstacles?

Who knows your struggles best?

1. **Matthew 16:18-** Hell will not overcome. My biggest fear is failure, but God already wipes out that option. He says Hell will not win.

2. **Mark 9:24-** I believe; help me overcome. Faith is so simple. Why can't we understand it?

3. **Luke 10:17-20-** Jesus gives us the authority to overcome. Thank you Jesus.

4. **John 16:33-** Jesus warns us of the troubles but He encourages us because He has overcome. It will not be easy to overcome but it is possible and guaranteed if we persevere.

5. **Romans 12:21-** Overcome evil with good. It's a simple plan.

6. **1 John 2:13-** You have already overcome. That's a reassuring scripture.

7. **1 John 4:4-** Since we are with God we overcome and only if we are with God do we overcome.

Pray: That you will not fall into temptation and you will overcome sin.

BECOME ONE

In step with the Spirit

Holy Spirit dwell in me;
Touch my eyes that I might see.
All your goodness grace and power
Stay beside me every hour
Be my drink, be my living bread
Keep me sheltered, keep me fed.
Holy Spirit, Holy Spirit dwell in me

Holy Spirit comfort me;
Let my heart be one with thee.
When I worry to my mind;
Let me sweet contentment find.
May I run this wicked race;
Fill me by your amazing grace.
Holy Spirit, Holy Spirit comfort me

Holy Spirit rescue me;
Set my soul completely free.
Be-side Jordan make my bed;
In God's bosom lay my head.
Let me live in a brand new place;
See my Blessed Savior's face.
Holy Spirit, Holy Spirit rescue me.

This can be a very difficult chapter for some people to understand and I know I cannot do it justice. I know everyone has a different experience with the Holy Spirit and that's the way it should be, but some people have had negative experiences or fake experiences. I am not, like the rest of the book, going to do an intense study of the Holy Ghost but I will try my best to explain it in two pages.

I want to focus the first page on Romans 8. The title is Life through the Spirit and that's what I want to talk about. It starts off by saying there is no condemnation in Christ. Why? Because that is why Christ came, He came to save us and to give us freedom. Christ came to fulfill the law for us and He did. He did so we could live. His blood continually washes away our sin, because we are always sinning. That's why we have to live in the Spirit because that is the way we keep in contact with His blood. Jesus is no longer here in body but He is here in Spirit. We need to be in that Spirit that washes away our sin.

Romans tells us that there is a battle between the sinful nature but if we live by the Spirit we do not live by sinful nature. Sin will dominate you if you live by the sinful nature. If your mind is controlled by the sinful nature you will die. Those who are under the sinful nature can never please God. It is like two dogs living in us, The Righteous one and the Sinful one. The one we feed the most will destroy the other.

We as Christians are controlled by the Spirit. It is not that we should be, it is that we are. If you are not in Christ you are not in the Spirit. I know some people reject the Spirit and some say you will get the Holy Spirit at a different time in your walk with God or some say all Christians do not get it. That's not what verse 9 says. If you are a Christian the Spirit of God is living in you. I didn't say if you attend church or if you are a nice person, if you are true disciple of Christ.

We do not have an obligation to the sinful nature. I feel bad for people who are not Christians because they have no other choice but to sin. They have an obligation. They really don't know what else to do. It is so hard to find good entertainment these days because most entertainers are non-Christian. Their clothes are sinful, the dancing is sinful, the jokes are sinful, the songs are sinful. It seems so difficult to enjoy good clean fun.

The Holy Spirit speaks deep in our hearts. Our conscience should bother us more as Christians. I did not struggle with certain things before I was a Christian because I just indulged in them. Now I am sensitive to sin because I am God's child and His Spirit whispers, "That's not good". And because we are God's children we get everything that is His, all of His treasures. It also means now that we are here in the flesh we also participate in His sufferings.

We are eagerly waiting for God's glory to be revealed. We have something to look forward to. I also think some people will be shocked because they were not living in the Spirit. (Matthew 7:21) This is not the fulfillment of what is promised on earth. Our hope is in heaven. We will get bummed out here but the Holy Spirit helps us in our distress. As longs as we stay in Christ, nothing can separate us from God's love.

I'm sure you have heard the expression "Go with the flow". I'm not too fond of that saying but when we don't know what's going on, or where to go, we just need to F.L.O.W. in the Spirit. Fear not, Let go, Open your heart, and Wait for God.

Let's look at some scriptures that will help us to FLOW with God. There is no fear in love (1 John 4:18-19) so we don't need to fear. We can just trust. He says I will never leave you. (Hebrews 13:5) He reminds us, I am with you always. (Matthew 28:19-20), So we can let go and let God. He's got it. He wants us to receive Him (John 1:12). We need to open our hearts to Him. In Acts 1:4 Jesus tells His disciples to wait for the Holy Spirit. We do not need to make any moves without the Holy Spirit; we see what happens in Acts 2. The Holy Spirit moves powerfully.

Chapters 14, 15, and 16 of John spend a lot time talking about the Holy Spirit. The New American Standard Version refers to the Holy Spirit as the Advocate. That's a cool concept - the Spirit is there for us. All three chapters focus remaining with God and we will always have His Advocate to back us up. John 15 gives the analogy of bearing fruit on the vine. We have to remain on the Jesus vine if we want the Spirit's fruits.

I want to end with a bunch of scriptures that relate to the Holy Spirit. I hope they will help you understand the Spirit a little more. Just understand you can never achieve the Spirit with our Human effort.

The Old Testament Spirit -Exodus 31:3 The Spirit will fill you with different skills and abilities. Numbers 11:25 The Spirit will move from one person to another. Judges 6:34 The Spirit was on Gideon. Judges 11:29 The Spirit was on Jeptha. Judges 13:25 The Spirit was on Samson. 1 Samuel 10:10 The Spirit came upon Saul with power. 2 Samuel 23:2 The Spirit of the Lord spoke through David. Job 33:4 The Spirit makes us breathe and gives us life.

The Psalms and Isaiah- Psalm 51:11 Do not take your Holy Spirit away from me. Psalms 106:33 They rebelled against the Spirit of God. Psalms 139:7 Where can I go from your Spirit? Isaiah 32:15 The Spirit is poured out from on high. Isaiah 61:1 The Spirit is on me to preach good news. Isaiah 63:10 They rebelled and grieved the Holy Spirit.

The Gospel Spirit- Matthew 1:18 and Luke 1:35, Jesus was born by the Holy Spirit. Matthew 3:11 You will get baptized with the Holy Spirit. Matthew 3:16 and Luke 4:18 Jesus was filled with the Holy Spirit. Matthew 10:20 We speak through the Spirit Matthew 12:31 Don't sin against the Spirit. Luke 11:13 Don't grieve the Spirit. John 6:63 The Spirit gives life. John 7:39 The Spirit came at a certain time. John 20:22 Breathe in the Spirit.

Pauline epistles Spirit -Galatians 3:2 the Holy Spirit does not come through the law. Ephesians 4:30 don't grieve the Holy Spirit, you are sealed with Him. Ephesians 5:18 Get drunk off of the Holy Spirit - it is a very wild feeling. Philippians 3:3 Worship in the Spirit

Your relationship with the Holy Spirit is personal. You are the only one who will be able to experience it for yourself. He is there to comfort us not to confuse us.

Do you feel the Holy Spirit in you?

Do you quench the Spirit?

What else do you want to know about the Holy Spirit?

1. **1 Corinthians 2:14-** The one without the Spirit does not think about the things the Spirit does.

2. **2 Corinthians 1:22-** He is deposit, our guarantee of ownership. We need that stamp to make it to heaven.

3. **Ephesians 1:13-** We also need the seal of the Spirit. There is only one real seal it's not something we could fake.

4. **Galatians 5:16-** Live by the Spirit and you will not sin. There is no law against the Holy Spirit.

5. **Galatians 5:22-** The fruits of the spirit are love, joy, peace, patience, kindness, goodness, faithfulness, self-control, and gentleness. Are you living like this?

6. **John 14:26-** The Counselor will teach us. We have someone to counsel, guide, direct, and protect us.

7. **John 16:13-** The Spirit speaks the truth of God. If we follow the Spirit we will not live a life of lies.

Pray: God empty my selfish desires and fill me with your Spirit.

ALMOST DONE

End times

Soon and very soon we are going to see the
king3x
Halleujah Halleujah we are going to see the king.

No more crying there were are going to see the
king 3x
Halleujah, Halleujah we are going to see the king

No more dying there we are going to see the
king 3x
Halleujah Halleujah we are going to see the king

Doomsday, Armageddon, The End of Times, The Last days, The Second Coming, whatever it is you want to call it. We have all talked about it, we have all thought about it. Are you scared about it? Are you excited about it? What will it be like? When will it be? It's so exhilarating. Don't you agree?

The thing is, we don't know when Jesus is coming. The Bible says He will come like a thief in the night. (1 Thessalonians 5:2) Some of us don't like that. We would like to know when it is coming. We don't like pop quizzes. We want to be prepared. But the thing is we can be prepared and we should be prepared.

Matthew 25: 10 gives us a perfect example of what that means. It is the story of the ten virgins. Only half of them were prepared. There was not enough oil to share. Just like there will not be enough faith to share on the last day. Not even between families. Each person will be judged for themselves. So what that means is we always need to be prepared all the time.

I am not too concerned when or how the end of days will be. Matthew 24 and Mark 13 tell us that the day and hour is unknown. So what can we do about it? I think it makes sense because my last day can be today. I might not even be able to finish this book. So, hey, I need to be prepared. I am flying on a plane again. I might not land. But I would feel great about going up to heaven if Jesus is ready to call me. I am with my wife and daughter. We can all go up to heaven together.

I think it is funny when people say we are in the End of Days. The same chapters in Matthew and Mark talk about that. I say it is funny because things have always been crazy. In the first century people were crucified and thrown into lions' dens. Look at the time of the Crusades, people were killed and raped and they were claiming it was for Christ. The times when our nation was being formed, we treated people as they were property . The drugs and wars of the 60s and 70s. We could go on and on about how we could say any one of those times were the end of times but we are still around and now we have the swine flu.

All of those times and more were the end of times for many people. Whenever God calls you is your end of times. But are there signs? Yeah, there are always signs. So again that means you always need to be prepared. I'm sure we will hear a lot of predictions and I believe they will be true for a lot of people. But as for me and my house we will be prepared, if the end comes in ten minutes, ten years, or ten decades.

Death is scary for a lot of people. I think the main reason is that it is so unknown. People say they have been to heaven and back. People claim to talk to the dead or say they have had dreams. To me and I think to most of you that is still very unclear. As Christians we need to be excited about death. It means that we are leaving these earthly sinful bodies and we are going to meet our Creator. Our whole Christian walk is based on faith. (Hebrews 11).

My wife and I also discuss how this life wouldn't be that bad even if there wasn't a heaven. If we died and that's it (which is not what I

164

believe) I wouldn't feel like I wasted my life living for Jesus. First of all we would be dead and we wouldn't be able to care. Second of all living as a Christian in the Spirit is awesome because we get a taste of heaven on earth.

We touched on this in the last chapter but it applies again in this chapter. Colossians 1:15 says we need to put our hope in Heaven. Hope is very powerful. If we are living for something we will live long and strong. I'm sure you remember the Lance Armstrong bands that say Live Strong. They supported cancer research. You can get very discouraged living with any disease. But those bands encourage people to live whatever life that they have left in them as strongly as they could.

I caught the end of the movie "Bicentennial Man" the other night. If you didn't see the movie it's basically about a robot who wants to become human. He gets married to a human and she tells him she is going die. That is the natural order of things. Since he was still a robot he was not going to die. So he said to his wife, if you die then I have no reason to live. Hope and purpose are powerful things. We all need something to live for. If we don't life becomes meaningless.

In my opinion if HOPE was an acronym it would stand for: Happy, Optimistic, Peaceful, and Eternal. Hope gives you a different perspective. You will be happy because you have a purpose. You are optimistic because you believe better things are to come. You are peaceful because His word gives you a sense of peace. And you think eternal because there is a sense of eternity in your heart and soul. (Ecc 3:11)

How can we have this hope? You need to trust in the Lord. (Proverbs 3:5-6). That's basically all we can do when we live in a world with so much uncertainty. We have been at war for way too long. It can be anytime that one of our enemies will launch some nuclear bomb. You can get into a car accident no matter how careful you are. Or you could just trip and fall. So how could we live a life that is not filled with fear? Trust in the Lord.

This is hard for people because they couldn't trust people in their life. People fail you. People lie to you. People hurt you. It is hard to trust people. God is not people. He can be trusted. He keeps the Earth spinning on it axis. He allows the sun to come up every morning. He keeps the whole universe in motion and perfect harmony. God can be trusted. Wherever you are in your trust with God, pray that you will learn to trust Him more.

We can't live our life in fear because death, hell, and suffering are all very scary things. The only way not to be afraid of those things is to hope and trust in something greater. So let's not build up our storehouse here and try and fill it up with the best stuff on earth (Luke 12:16-21) because God has greater things in store for us.

Your time can come at any moment. I don't know what it will look like and neither do you. We have all the signs of the end of times. There is nothing more to look for. Things could get better or things could worse. But you need to be prepared for whatever will come.

Do you look forward to dying?

What do you want to accomplish before you go?

Write a letter to God. What did it say?

1. **Luke 13: 32-** Jesus was focused on His goal. His Goal was to die for YOU!

2. **Galatians 3:3-** We cannot achieve our goal by human effort. God has given us what we need to accomplish our goal.

3. **Philippians 3:12-14-** God has the prize so we press on towards our goal.

4. **1 Timothy 1:5-** The Goal is Love because God is Love.

5. **1 Peter 1:9-** Salvation of our souls is the goal of our faith. These bodies will die but are souls will last forever. Where is your soul headed?

6. **Luke 21:5-36-** Jesus speaks of the end of the age. It is easy to say that we are in the end of days right now.

7. **Luke 12-** Jesus warns and encourages, He teaches about not storing up the wrong things, He tells us not to worry, He says be watchful, He said there will be fire, and He also gives us many other specific visuals.

Pray: Let me live today as if it were my last day on earth.

YOU'VE WON

Praise God

Stand in awe your power and your glory
Stand in awe with trembling and fear
Stand in awe you're sovereign and you're holy
Lord oh God we stand in awe

Your deeds your name your works of creation
Your love your law your plan of salvation
The stars seem unnumbered the lightning the thunder the
universe under your reign

Stand in awe your power and your glory
Stand in awe with trembling and fear
Stand in awe you're sovereign and you're holy
Lord oh God we stand in awe

We stand in Christ as your holy nation
We take your word to our generation.
Your hand is upon us your spirit within us and hell can't
prevent us we've won! We've won!

Stand in awe your power and your glory
Stand in awe with trembling and fear
Stand in awe you're sovereign and you're holy
Lord oh God we stand in awe!

It is finished!

Isn't it an awesome feeling to get something accomplished? Today was the last day of school. What an awesome feeling. You graduated! Doesn't it feel great to finish a puzzle or some other art project you were working on? My friend was working on a puzzle and someone finished it for her without permission. It's not the same feeling when someone else finishes for you. I mentioned the Olympics in one of the previous chapters. Imagine how good it must feel to win a gold medal. That says you are the best in the world.

To win is the goal. We don't want to live this life and end up as a loser. Now if you choose to be on Christ's team you are already a winner. Jesus said it is finished. (John 19:30) He has already defeated Satan. You just need to stay on His team and you win. For me just making it to the Olympics would classify me as a winner. Jesus treats you like a winner if you are on His team.

I hope you read through this book in order and this is your last chapter, so you can say I am done. "I finished the book." It is a good feeling just to finish the book. But there was a goal, a goal to get closer to God. Hopefully you accomplished that also. Now you won't look any different or smell any different if you are closer to God. You just become more different.

Now is not a time to get discouraged or down but a time to rejoice. You always have to evaluate yourself and test yourself, but you can also encourage yourself and thank God that He saved a sinner like you. Thank God for giving you an opportunity to be on the winning team. You can go to sleep each night and say I've won. If you are still in Christ you are a winner.

As Christians we can live every day with hope and without fear. Relax. God is in control. More Christians need to walk around with confidence as winners, no longer as sinners. We once were sinners, now we are saved by grace. Rejoice and continue growing closer to God. Keep on taking those steps. Today may be your last one or you can have trillions more to go. But whatever you do take those steps in Christ because if you do, you already know the outcome. You've WON!

John tells us at the end of his Gospel that there is not enough room in this world if we would try to write about all the great things about Jesus. I definitely feel the same way as I am writing now. I can keep writing and writing. I can keep changing my thoughts or my phrases. Even if I don't stop writing or thinking or reading, I will never be able to grasp how deep, how wide and how far God's love is for me. So we keep on walking. Closer and closer, day by day, we take our time to reflect, repent, and revere.

This is not the end, you are just getting started. Thank you so much for taking the journey with me. But most of all God is grateful that you chose to walk towards Him and His Son. Pray for me as I pray for you. I hope to see you soon in person or in Heaven Let's gather as many as we can to join us on the way. To God be the glory, forever and ever. Amen.

Are you Fired Up that you are Victorious in Christ?

How will your life be different?

Praise God!

Let's end with a scripture from each book of the New Testament.

- Matthew 5:3 Blessed are the poor in spirit, for theirs is the kingdom of heaven
- Mark 1:11 And a voice came from heaven: "You are my Son, whom I love; with you I am well pleased."
- Luke 6:23 Rejoice in that day and leap for joy, because great is your reward in heaven. For that is how their fathers treated the prophets.
- John 3:13 No one has ever gone into heaven except the one who came from heaven—the Son of Man
- Acts 3:21 He must remain in heaven until the time comes for God to restore everything, as he promise
- Romans 1:18 The wrath of God is being revealed from heaven against all the godlessness and wickedness of men who suppress the truth by their wickedness long ago through his holy prophets
- 1 Corinthians 15:49 And just as we have borne the likeness of the earthly man, so shall we bear the likeness of the man from heaven.
- 2 Corinthians 5:1 [*Our Heavenly Dwelling*] Now we know that if the earthly tent we live in is destroyed, we have a building from God, an eternal house in heaven, not built by human hands
- Galatians 1:8 But even if we or an angel from heaven should preach a gospel other than the one we preached to you, let him be eternally condemned!
- Ephesians 1:10 to be put into effect when the times will have reached their fulfillment—to bring all things in heaven and on earth together under one head, even Christ
- Philippians 3:20 But our citizenship is in heaven. And we eagerly await a Savior from there, the Lord Jesus Christ
- Colossians 4:1 Masters, provide your slaves with what is right and fair, because you know that you also have a Master in heaven.
- 1 Thessalonians 1:10 and to wait for his Son from heaven, whom he raised from the dead—Jesus, who rescues us from the coming wrath.
- 2 Thessalonians 1:7 and give relief to you who are troubled, and to us as well. This will happen when the Lord Jesus is revealed from heaven in blazing fire with his powerful angels.
- 1 Timothy 1:15 Christ Jesus came into this world to save sinners

- 2 Timothy 4:18 The Lord will rescue me from every evil attack and will bring me safely to his heavenly kingdom. To him be glory for ever and ever. Amen
- Titus 3:7 We might become heirs having the hope of eternal life
- Philemon 22 Prepare a guest room for me, because I hope to be restored to you in answer to your prayer
- Hebrews 8:5 They serve at a sanctuary that is a copy and shadow of what is in heaven. This is why Moses was warned when he was about to build the tabernacle: "See to it that you make everything according to the pattern shown you on the mountain."
- James 3:17 But the wisdom that comes from heaven is first of all pure; then peace-loving, considerate, submissive, full of mercy and good fruit, impartial and sincere
- 1 Peter 1:12 It was revealed to them that they were not serving themselves but you, when they spoke of the things that have now been told you by those who have preached the gospel to you by the Holy Spirit sent from heaven. Even angels long to look into these things.
- 2 Peter 3:13 But in keeping with his promise we are looking forward to a new heaven and a new earth, the home of righteousness.
- 1 John 2:17 The world and its desires pass away, but the man who does the will of God lives forever
- 2 John 2 the truth, which lives in us, will be with us forever.
- 3 John 4 I have no greater joy than to hear that my children are walking in the truth.
- Jude 21 Keep yourself in God's love as you wait for the mercy of our Lord Jesus Christ to bring you to eternal life.
- Revelation 4:1 [The *Throne in Heaven*] After this I looked, and there before me was a door standing open in heaven. And the voice I had first heard speaking to me like a trumpet said, "Come up here, and I will show you what must take place after this."

The beginning!

1. Genesis 7:12 And rain fell on the earth forty days and forty nights.

2. Genesis 25:20 and Isaac was forty years old when he married Rebekah

3. Genesis 50:3 taking a full forty days, for that was the time required for embalming

4. Exodus 16:35 The Israelites ate manna forty years

5. Exodus 24:18 Then Moses entered the cloud as he went on up the mountain. And he stayed on the mountain forty days and forty nights.

6. Exodus 34:28 Moses was there with the LORD forty days and forty nights without eating bread or drinking water. And he wrote on the tablets the words of the covenant—the Ten Commandments.

7. Numbers 13:25 At the end of forty days they returned from exploring the land.

8. Numbers 14:33 Your children will be shepherds here for forty years, suffering for your unfaithfulness, until the last of your bodies lies in the desert.

9. Numbers 32:13 The Lord's anger burned against Israel and he made them wander in the desert forty years, until the whole generation of those who had done evil in his sight was gone.

10. Deuteronomy 2:7 The LORD your God has blessed you in all the work of your hands. He has watched over your journey through this vast desert. These forty years the LORD your God has been with you, and you have not lacked anything.

11. Deuteronomy 25:3 but he must not give him more than forty lashes. If he is flogged more than that, your brother will be degraded in your eyes.

12. Joshua 14:7I was forty years old when Moses the servant of the LORD sent me from Kadesh Barnea to explore the land. And I brought him back a report according to my convictions, (Caleb)

13. Judges 3:11 So the land had peace for forty years, until Othniel son of Kenaz died.

14. Judges 5:31 "So may all your enemies perish, O LORD! But may they who love you be like the sun when it rises in its strength." Then the land had peace forty years.

15. Judges 8:28 [Gideon's Death] Thus Midian was subdued before the Israelites and did not raise its head again. During Gideon's lifetime, the land enjoyed peace forty years.

16. Judges 13:1 [The Birth of Samson] Again the Israelites did evil in the eyes of the LORD, so the LORD delivered them into the hands of the Philistines for forty years.

17. 1 Samuel 17:16 For forty days the Philistine came forward every morning and evening and took his stand.

18. 2 Samuel 5:4 David was thirty years old when he became king, and he reigned forty years.

19. 1 Kings 11:42 Solomon reigned in Jerusalem over all Israel forty years.

20. 1 Kings 19:8 So he got up and ate and drank. Strengthened by that food, he traveled forty days and forty nights until he reached Horeb, the mountain of God. (Elijah)

21. 2 Kings 12:1 [Joash Repairs the Temple] In the seventh year of Jehu, Joash became king, and he reigned in Jerusalem forty years. His mother's name was Zibiah; she was from Beersheba.

22. Ezekiel 29:13 " 'Yet this is what the Sovereign LORD says: At the end of forty years I will gather the Egyptians from the nations where they were scattered.

23. Jonah 3:4 On the first day, Jonah started into the city. He proclaimed: "Forty more days and Nineveh will be overturned."

24. Matthew 4:2 After fasting forty days and forty nights, he was hungry.

25. Mark 1:13 and he was in the desert forty days, being tempted by Satan. He was with the wild animals, and angels attended him.

26. Luke 4:2 where for forty days he was tempted by the devil. He ate nothing during those days, and at the end of them he was hungry.

27. John 2:20 The Jews replied, "It has taken forty-six years to build this temple, and you are going to raise it in three days?"

28. Acts 1:3 After his suffering, he showed himself to these men and gave many convincing proofs that he was alive. He appeared to them over a period of forty days and spoke about the kingdom of God.

29. Acts 4:22 For the man who was miraculously healed was over forty years old.

30. Acts 7:23 "When Moses was forty years old, he decided to visit his fellow Israelites.

31. Acts 7:30 "After forty years had passed, an angel appeared to Moses in the flames of a burning bush in the desert near Mount Sinai

32. Acts 7:36 He led them out of Egypt and did wonders and miraculous signs in Egypt, at the Red Sea and for forty years in the desert.

33. Acts 7:42 But God turned away and gave them over to the worship of the heavenly bodies. This agrees with what is written in the book of the prophets: " 'Did you bring me sacrifices and offerings forty years in the desert, O house of Israel?

34. Acts 13:18 he endured their conduct for about forty years in the desert,

35. Acts 13:21 "After this, God gave them judges until the time of Samuel the prophet. Then the people asked for a king, and he gave them Saul son of Kish, of the tribe of Benjamin, who ruled forty years.

36. Acts 23:13 More than forty men were involved in this plot.

37. Acts 23:21 Don't give in to them, because more than forty of them are waiting in ambush for him. They have taken an oath not to eat or drink until they have killed him. They are ready now, waiting for your consent to their request."

38. 2 Corinthians 11:24 Five times I received from the Jews the forty lashes minus one.

39. Hebrews 3:9 where your fathers tested and tried me and for forty years saw what I did.

40. Hebrews 3:17 And with whom was he angry for forty years? Was it not with those who sinned, whose bodies fell in the desert?

The Names of God

by Lambert Dolphin ldolphin.org

Old Testament (The Hebrew Scriptures, or Tanach):

1 - EL: אֵל God ("mighty, strong, prominent") used 250 times in the OT
See Gen. 7:1, 28:3, 35:11; Nu. 23:22; Josh. 3:10; 2 Sam. 22:31, 32; Neh.
1:5, 9:32; Isa. 9:6; Ezek. 10:5. El is linguistically equivalent to the Moslem
"Allah," but the attributes of Allah in Islam are entirely different from
those of the God of the Hebrews. ELAH is Aramaic, "god." Elah appears
in the Hebrew Bible in Jer. 10:11 (which is in Aramaic, and is plural,
"gods"). In Daniel (the Aramaic sections) Elah is used both of pagan gods,
and of the true God, also plural. Elah is equivalent to the Hebrew Eloah
which some think is dual; Elohim is three or more. The gods of the nations
are called "elohim." The origin of Eloah is obscure. Elohim is the more
common plural form of El. Eloah is used 41 times in Job between 3:4 and
40:2, but fewer than 15 times elsewhere in the OT.

2 - ELOHIM: אֱלֹהִים God (a plural noun, more than two, used with
singular verbs); Elohim occurs 2,570 times in the OT, 32 times in Gen. 1.
God as Creator, Preserver, Transcendent, Mighty and Strong. Eccl., Dan.
Jonah use Elohim almost exclusively. See Gen. 17:7, 6:18, 9:15, 50:24; I
Kings 8:23; Jer. 31:33; Isa. 40:1.

3 - EL SHADDAI: אֵל שַׁדַּי God Almighty or "God All Sufficient."
48 times in the OT, 31 times in Job. First used in Gen. 17:1, 2. (Gen.
31:29, 49:24, 25; Prov. 3:27; Micah 2:1; Isa. 60:15, 16, 66:10-13; Ruth
1:20, 21) In Rev. 16:7, "Lord God the Almighty." The Septuagint uses
Greek "ikanos" meaning "all-sufficient" or "self-sufficient." The idols of
the heathen are called "sheddim."

4 - ADONAI: אֲדֹנָי Lord in our English Bibles (Capitol letter 'L ',
lower case, 'ord') (Adonai is plural, the sing. is "adon"). "Master" or "Lord"
300 times in the OT always plural when referring to God, when sing. the
reference is to a human lord. Used 215 times to refer to men. First use of
Adonai, Gen. 15:2. (Ex. 4:10; Judges 6:15; 2 Sam. 7:18-20; Ps. 8, 114:7,
135:5, 141:8, 109:21-28). Heavy use in Isaiah (Adonai Jehovah). 200 times
by Ezekiel. Ten times in Dan. 9.

174

5 - JEHOVAH: יְהוָה LORD in our English Bibles (all capitals). Yahweh is the covenant name of God. Occurs 6823 times in the OT First use Gen. 2:4 (Jehovah Elohim). From the verb "to be", havah, similar to chavah (to live), "The Self-Existent One," "I AM WHO I AM" or 'I WILL BE WHO I WILL BE" as revealed to Moses at the burning bush, Ex.3. The name of God, too sacred to be uttered, abbreviated (. . . .) or written "YHWH" without vowel points. The tetragrammaton. Josh., Judges, Sam., and Kings use Jehovah almost exclusively. The love of God is conditioned upon His moral and spiritual attributes. (Dan. 9:14; Ps. 11:7; Lev. 19:2; Hab. 1:12). Note Deut. 6:4, 5 known to Jews as the Sh'ma uses both Jehovah and Elohim to indicate one God with a plurality of persons.

6 - JEHOVAH-JIREH: יְהוָה יִרְאֶה "The Lord will Provide." Gen. 22:14. From "jireh" ("to see" or "to provide," or to "foresee" as a prophet.) God always provides, adequate when the times come.

7 - JEHOVAH-ROPHE: יְהוָה רֹפֵא "The Lord Who Heals" Ex. 15:22-26. From "rophe" ("to heal"); implies spiritual, emotional as well as physical healing. (Jer. 30:17, 3:22; Isa. 61:1) God heals body, soul and spirit; all levels of man's being.

8 - JEHOVAH-NISSI: יְהוָה נִסִּי "The Lord Our Banner." Ex. 17:15. God on the battlefield, from word which means "to glisten," "to lift up," See Psalm 4:6.

9 - JEHOVAH-M'KADDESH: יְהוָה קָדַשׁ "The Lord Who Sanctifies" Lev. 20:8. "To make whole, set apart for holiness."

10 - JEHOVAH-SHALOM: יְהוָה שָׁלוֹם "The Lord Our Peace" Judges 6:24. "Shalom" translated "peace" 170 times means "whole," "finished," "fulfilled," "perfected." Related to "well," welfare." Deut. 27:6; Dan. 5:26; I Kings 9:25 8:61; Gen. 15:16; Ex. 21:34, 22:5, 6; Lev. 7:11-21. Shalom means that kind of peace that results from being a whole person in right relationship to God and to one's fellow man.

11 - SHEPHERD: רֹעֶה Psa. 23, 79:13, 95:7, 80:1, 100:3; Gen. 49:24; Isa. 40:11.

12 - JUDGE: שֹׁפֵט Psa. 7:8, 96:13.

13 - JEHOVAH ELOHIM: יהוה אלהים "LORD God" Gen. 2:4; Judges 5:3; Isa. 17:6; Zeph. 2:9; Psa. 59:5, etc.

14 - JEHOVAH-TSIDKENU יהוה צדקנו "The Lord Our Righteousness" Jer. 23:5, 6, 33:16. From "tsidek" (straight, stiff, balanced - as on scales - full weight, justice, right, righteous, declared innocent.) God our Righteousness.

15 - JEHOVAH-ROHI: יהוה רעה "The Lord Our Shepherd" Psa. 23, from "ro'eh" (to pasture).

16 - JEHOVAH-SHAMMAH: יהוה שמה "The Lord is There" (Ezek. 48:35).

17 - JEHOVAH-SABAOTH: יהוה צבא "The Lord of Hosts" The commander of the angelic host and the armies of God. Isa. 1:24; Psa. 46:7, 11; 2 Kings 3:9-12; Jer. 11:20 (NT: Rom. 9:29; James 5:4, Rev. 19: 11-16).

18 - EL ELYON: אל עליון 'Most High" (from "to go up") Deut. 26:19, 32:8; Psa. 18:13; Gen. 14:18; Nu. 24:16; Psa. 78:35, 7:17, 18:13, 97:9, 56:2, 78:56, 18:13; Dan. 7:25, 27; Isa. 14:14.

19 - ABHIR: אביד 'Mighty One', ("to be strong") Gen. 49:24; Deut. 10:17; Psa. 132:2, 5; Isa. 1:24, 49:26, 60:1.

20 - BRANCH: צמח (tsemach), The Branch: Zech. 3:8, 6:12; Isa. 4:2; Jer. 23:5, 33:15.

21 - KADOSH: קדוש "Holy One" Psa. 71:22; Isa. 40:25, 43:3, 48:17. Isaiah uses the expression "the Holy One of Israel" 29 times.

22 - SHAPHAT: שפטש "Judge" Gen. 18:25

176

23 - EL ROI: **אל ראי** "God of Seeing" Hagar in Gen. 16:13. The God Who opens our eyes.

24 - KANNA: **קנא** "Jealous" (zealous). Ex. 20:5, 34:14; Deut. 5:9; Isa. 9:7; Zech. 1:14, 8:2.

25 - PALET: **פלט** "Deliverer" Psa. 18:2.

26 - YESHUA: **ישׁוּע** (Yeshua) "Savior" ("he will save"). Isa. 43:3. Jesus is the Greek equivalent of the Hebrew "Joshua." The latter is a contraction of Je-Hoshua. ("Christ", the anointed one is equivalent to the Hebrew Maschiah, or Messiah).

27 - GAOL: **גאל** "Redeemer" (to buy back by paying a price). Job 19:25; For example, the antitype corresponding to Boaz the Kinsman-Redeemer in the Book of Ruth.

28 - MAGEN: **מגן** "Shield" Psa. 3:3, 18:30.

29 - STONE: **אבן** Gen. 49:24

30 - EYALUTH: **אילות** "Strength" Psa. 22:19.

31 - TSADDIQ: **צדיק** "Righteous One" Psa. 7:9.

32 - EL-OLAM: **אל עולם** "Everlasting God" (God of everlasting time) Gen. 21:33; Psa. 90:1-3, 93:2; Isa. 26:4.

33 - EL-BERITH: **אל ברית** "God of the Covenant" Used of Baal in Judges 9:46. Probably used originally to refer to the God of Israel.

34 - EL-GIBHOR: **אל גבור** Mighty God (Isa. 9:6)

35 - ZUR: **צור** "God our Rock" Deut. 32:18; Isa. 30:29.

Malachi calls Messiah "The Sun of Righteousness" (Malachi 4:2).

Isaiah calls Messiah "Wonderful, Counselor, Mighty God (El Gibhor), Everlasting Father, Prince of Peace" (Isa. 9:6).

'Attiq Yomin (Aramaic): "Ancient of Days," Dan. 7:9, 13, 22.

36 - MELEKH: מלך "King" Psa. 5:2, 29:10, 44:4, 47:6-8, 48:2, 68:24, 74:12, 95:3, 97:1, 99:4, 146:10; Isa. 5:1, 5, 41:21, 43:15, 44:6; 52:7, 52:10.

"The Angel of the Lord: " Gen. 16:7ff, 21:17, 22:11, 15ff, 18:1-19:1, 24:7, 40, 31:11-13, 32:24-30; Ex. 3:6, 13:21, Ezek. 1:10-13. Seen in the theophanies, or pre-incarnate appearances of the Son of God in the OT (See I Cor. 10:3 NT).

37 - FATHER: אב 2 Sam. 7:14-15; Psa. 68:5; Isa. 63:16, 64:8; Mal. 1:6.

38 - THE FIRST AND LAST: Isa. 44:6, 48:12.

New Testament Scriptures, (Greek):

39 - KURIOS: (kurios) "Lord" Found some 600 times in the NT.

40 - THEOS: (yeos) "God" (equivalent to the Hebrew Elohim), 1,000 times in the NT. In the NT all the persons of the trinity are called "God" at one time or another.

For more information or to post a question or comment
Visit our website at www.James117Creations.com
Check out our other products and give us ideas of what
you would like to see in the future.
We would love to hear from you.

Breinigsville, PA USA
13 September 2009
223938BV00001B/1/P